**INTRODUCING
ISSUES WITH
OPPOSING
VIEWPOINTS®**

Athletes and Drug Use

David Haugen and Susan Musser, *Book Editors*

GREENHAVEN PRESS
A part of Gale, Cengage Learning

GALE
CENGAGE Learning·

Detroit • New York • San Francisco • New Haven, Conn • Waterville, Maine • London

Elizabeth Des Chenes, *Director, Publishing Solutions*

For more information, contact:
Greenhaven Press
27500 Drake Rd.
Farmington Hills, MI 48331-3535
Or you can visit our Internet site at gale.cengage.com

For product information and technology assistance, contact us at

Gale Customer Support, 1-800-877-4253
For permission to use material from this text or product, submit all requests online at
www.cengage.com/permissions

Further permissions questions can be e-mailed to permissionrequest@cengage.com

Articles in Greenhaven Press anthologies are often edited for length to meet page requirements. In addition, original titles of these works are changed to clearly present the main thesis and to explicitly indicate the author's opinion. Every effort is made to ensure that Greenhaven Press accurately reflects the original intent of the authors. Every effort has been made to trace the owners of copyrighted material.

Cover image © LiquidLibrary/Jupiterimages/Getty Images.

LIBRARY OF CONGRESS CATALOGING-IN-PUBLICATION DATA

Athletes and drug use / David Haugen and Susan Musser, book editors.
    p. cm. -- (Introducing issues with opposing viewpoints)
  Includes bibliographical references and index.
  ISBN 978-0-7377-6272-3 (hardcover)
  1. Athletes--Drug use. 2. Doping in sports. I. Haugen, David M., 1969- II. Musser, Susan.
  RC1230.A865 2012
  362.29--dc23

                                                                                        2012013294

Printed in the United States of America
1 2 3 4 5 6 7 16 15 14 13 12

Foreword

Introduction

Chapter 3: Is Drug Testing for Student Athletes Necessary and Effective?

Foreword

I ndulging in a wide spectrum of ideas, beliefs, and perspectives is a critical cornerstone of democracy. After all, it is often debates over differences of opinion, such as whether to legalize abortion, how to treat prisoners, or when to enact the death penalty, that shape our society and drive it forward. Such diversity of thought is frequently regarded as the hallmark of a healthy and civilized culture. As the Reverend Clifford Schutjer of the First Congregational Church in Mansfield, Ohio, declared in a 2001 sermon, "Surrounding oneself with only like-minded people, restricting what we listen to or read only to what we find agreeable is irresponsible. Refusing to entertain doubts once we make up our minds is a subtle but deadly form of arrogance." With this advice in mind, Introducing Issues with Opposing Viewpoints books aim to open readers' minds to the critically divergent views that comprise our world's most important debates.

Introducing Issues with Opposing Viewpoints simplifies for students the enormous and often overwhelming mass of material now available via print and electronic media. Collected in every volume is an array of opinions that captures the essence of a particular controversy or topic. Introducing Issues with Opposing Viewpoints books embody the spirit of nineteenth-century journalist Charles A. Dana's axiom: "Fight for your opinions, but do not believe that they contain the whole truth, or the only truth." Absorbing such contrasting opinions teaches students to analyze the strength of an argument and compare it to its opposition. From this process readers can inform and strengthen their own opinions, or be exposed to new information that will change their minds. Introducing Issues with Opposing Viewpoints is a mosaic of different voices. The authors are statesmen, pundits, academics, journalists, corporations, and ordinary people who have felt compelled to share their experiences and ideas in a public forum. Their words have been collected from newspapers, journals, books, speeches, interviews, and the Internet, the fastest growing body of opinionated material in the world.

Introducing Issues with Opposing Viewpoints shares many of the well-known features of its critically acclaimed parent series, Opposing Viewpoints. The articles are presented in a pro/con format, allowing readers to absorb divergent perspectives side by side. Active reading questions preface each viewpoint, requiring the student to approach the material thoughtfully and carefully. Useful charts, graphs, and cartoons supplement each article. A thorough introduction provides readers with crucial background on an issue. An annotated bibliography points the reader toward articles, books, and websites that contain additional information on the topic. An appendix of organizations to contact contains a wide variety of charities, nonprofit organizations, political groups, and private enterprises that each hold a position on the issue at hand. Finally, a comprehensive index allows readers to locate content quickly and efficiently.

Introducing Issues with Opposing Viewpoints is also significantly different from Opposing Viewpoints. As the series title implies, its presentation will help introduce students to the concept of opposing viewpoints and learn to use this material to aid in critical writing and debate. The series' four-color, accessible format makes the books attractive and inviting to readers of all levels. In addition, each viewpoint has been carefully edited to maximize a reader's understanding of the content. Short but thorough viewpoints capture the essence of an argument. A substantial, thought-provoking essay question placed at the end of each viewpoint asks the student to further investigate the issues raised in the viewpoint, compare and contrast two authors' arguments, or consider how one might go about forming an opinion on the topic at hand. Each viewpoint contains sidebars that include at-a-glance information and handy statistics. A Facts About section located in the back of the book further supplies students with relevant facts and figures.

Following in the tradition of the Opposing Viewpoints series, Greenhaven Press continues to provide readers with invaluable exposure to the controversial issues that shape our world. As John Stuart Mill once wrote: "The only way in which a human being can make some approach to knowing the whole of a subject is by hearing what can be said about it by persons of every variety of opinion and studying all modes in which it can be looked at by every character of mind. No wise man ever acquired his wisdom in any mode but this." It is to this principle that Introducing Issues with Opposing Viewpoints books are dedicated.

Introduction

Almost every major national and international sports association has banned the use of performance-enhancing drugs by athletes in competition. Claiming that performance enhancers give an unfair advantage to users, these organizations have prohibited steroids, growth hormones, amphetamines, painkillers, and other drugs for the variety of supposedly unfair benefits they afford athletes. In 1999 the International Olympic Committee and numerous governments established the World Anti-Doping Agency (WADA) to monitor and test athletes for drug use, and in 2004 WADA produced a written code—including a list of banned drugs, the methods of randomized testing, and the penalties for violations—that most sporting groups quickly adopted so that all athletes would be subject to the same restrictions. Even with the backing of sports authorities and the oversight of WADA, however, athletes continue to use outlawed drugs to build muscle, focus attention, increase endurance, and gain any other advantage possible within their field. According to a January 19, 2010, post on the Olympics news website, Around the Rings, German researchers concluded that perhaps 8 percent of Olympic athletes may be illegally doping—a number far higher than WADA's presumed 2 percent.

The number of high-profile doping cases in sports seems to confirm that the problem is fairly widespread. In April 2011 former San Francisco Giants outfielder and slugger Barry Bonds was convicted of obstructing justice and impeding a grand jury investigation of drugs in sports. Bonds, who had been snared in a probe seven years earlier after failing a drug test, declared his innocence, but prosecutors insisted he lied under oath about knowingly injecting steroids. The same month of Bonds's conviction, Tampa Bay outfielder and home run hitter Manny Ramirez retired from baseball after failing a drug test that would have resulted in a one-hundred-game suspension.

American football has also witnessed its share of drug violations. In 2007 New England Patriots strong safety Rodney Harrison was suspended from four games after admitting to using human growth hormone as a healing agent. The following year, the National Football League rounded up eight players for drug violations—though each has denied wrongdoing, claiming the illicit drugs were part of dietary supplements they presumed were harmless. Indeed, many athletes charged with drug violations argue that the substances were taken unknowingly as part of weight-loss aids or other common treatments.

The difficulty in assigning blame to athletes found with illicit substances in their bodies is one basis for questioning the fairness of drug policy. In an August 8, 2007, article for the *Doping Journal,* Anthony P. Millar points out that many athletes simply take painkillers, dietary aids, and other drugs to repair physical damage or to treat ailments. Contending that punishing such athletes seems unjust, Millar writes, "Athletes who have a medical problem are unfairly treated as they cannot follow the best therapeutic path for their illness. There is much confusion here. The authorities want to punish everyone to ensure that the guilty do not escape." However, beyond the potential to entrap the innocent, critics also argue that the desire to single out drugs as performance enhancers may be unreasonable. In a November 2005 article for *USA Today*, Matthew J. Mitten writes, "Virtually all athletes use various artificial means to enhance their body's natural performance while playing their respective sports." Mitten claims that diets, energy drinks, and even the design of specific equipment are engineered to create an advantage, so he wonders why authorities pick on drugs as worthy of banishment. He asks, "Is there really an appropriate line that can be drawn between legitimate athletic performance enhancement through artificial means and unethical doping to achieve an unfair competitive advantage? For example, athletes' usage of artificially created low-oxygen living environments in low-altitude training areas currently is permitted, whereas their use of erythropoietin (EPO) [a drug that increases red blood cell count and thus oxygen-carrying capacity] to achieve similar effects is prohibited by sports governing bodies."

Defenders of antidoping strategies in sports, though, believe that a line has been crossed by those taking performance-enhancing drugs. In a June 27, 2008, *New York Times* interview, Gary Wadler, chairman of the World Anti-Doping Agency's Prohibited List and Methods Committee, insists, "Sport is a contest in character, not in chemistry or pharmacology. Not only is doping dangerous to one's health, it blatantly violates the spirit of sport." Wadler goes on to stipulate that all sports are governed by rules, and if players do not wish to conform to the rules, then they do not belong in competition. Michele Verroken, a key developer of the United Kingdom's antidoping policy in sports, similarly argued that these laws are in place to guarantee the integrity of those athletes who wish to compete fairly and by the rules. Quoted in a November 15, 2001, press release from UK Sport, the British government's sporting authority, Verroken stated, "Whilst many people may assume that the purpose of our fight against drugs in sport is to catch athletes who are cheating, ultimately it is as much about protecting the reputations of those who are determined to be drug free."

The practicality of drug testing methods and the ethical questions that pertain to the notion of banning performance-enhancing drugs in sports are examined within this anthology, *Introducing Issues with Opposing Viewpoints: Athletes and Drug Use*. Offering a variety of perspectives on this issue, the authors featured in this volume debate the merits of drug bans, the appropriate consequences for violations, and the justification for extending drug testing to student athletes.

Chapter 1

Should Performance-Enhancing Drugs Be Tolerated in Sports?

The use of performance-enhancing drugs for athletes in sports has caused controversy in the athletic world.

Performance-Enhancing Drugs Ruin the Fairness of Sports

"Playing to the rules is paramount in any sport and cheating by taking performance enhancing drugs to gain an unfair advantage just isn't on."

Johnny O'Connor

In the following viewpoint, United Kingdom rugby player and athletic coach Johnny O'Connor argues that performance-enhancing drugs are banned in sports to level the playing field and ensure that talent and perseverance define winning athletes. O'Connor claims drugs ruin competition by giving some athletes an unfair advantage; he believes that hard work and courage are what sports demand. In addition, O'Connor insists that aderence to no-drug policies keep alive the sense of admiration that both audiences and other athletes hold for those sports figures who overcome the challenges of competition without drugs or other questionable advantages.

AS YOU READ, CONSIDER THE FOLLOWING QUESTIONS:

1. What are the six factors that O'Connor names as keys to success in sports?
2. What is the overriding concern O'Connor has in making his argument for not allowing athletes to make their own decisions about what supplements they should and should not take?
3. According to the author, why does the sport of cycling seem to suffer so many accusations of drug use among its participants?

The use of performance-enhancing drugs in sport is a very controversial topic. Because it has been so prevalent in sport in recent years, you might find yourself asking if it would be better if everyone was allowed to use them in order to maximise their genetic potential.

It's something that was brought up by Simon Barnes, the Chief Sports Writer with *The Times,* a few years back when he was covering the Beijing Olympics [in 2008]. It's a controversial suggestion I know, but thanks to constant testing by WADA (World Anti-Doping Agency) it's not an option and we should be grateful for it because athletes need to be protected from themselves in sport.

Whatever about illegal substances, it is clear that there is already a problem with legalised supplements because people abuse them through overuse and damage their health as a result. Legalising performance-enhancing drugs gives people a false pretense of exactly what it takes to succeed at the highest level in sport. Improving physically whilst you have the skillset will help, but it is only one part of the success.

Success in sport also requires raw talent, dedication, knowledge, coaching and desire. I feel if everyone was allowed to take drugs and did in fact take drugs, you would still have the same people at the top of their game in sports such as sprinting, swimming, rugby, etc., because it's the competitors with the greatest amount of the qualities listed above that always seem to rise to the top.

Fair Competitions

I agree with doping testing because there has to be fairness in sport for both the participants and the spectators/supporters. Respect is also vital and mutual respect amongst players is key—if a team knows one player is getting an unfair advantage, team morale is reduced, as is trust amongst the players.

The same applies to individual sports—if the person in the lane beside you is taking drugs, why should they be allowed to get away

Proponents of drug testing for athletes say testing is necessary to ensure that sports competitions are fair.

with an unfair advantage? A uniform ban on performance enhancing drugs is paramount to the survival and continued success of all sports. Even though everyone knows it's wrong, there are still people who will take the risk and still cheat, but constant regulation acts as a huge deterrent.

But is there anything to be said for a different stance that would allow performance enhancing drugs to be used across the board?

You could argue that it allows for complete transparency within the sporting industry—all athletes are allowed [to] take drugs, everybody has equal access to them and in return they will reap or suffer the consequences of their decision. From a spectator's viewpoint, they are aware of the athletes' access to drugs and if they knew what was going on, their interest and following of a sport might not decline as a result.

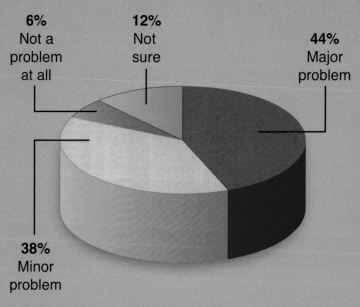

Nearly Half of Americans Polled Think the Use of Performance-Enhancing Drugs Is a Major Problem

Do you think the use of steroids and other performance-enhancing drugs by professional atheletes is a major problem or not?

6%
Not a
problem
at all

12%
Not
sure

44%
Major
problem

38%
Minor
problem

Taken from: Economist/YouGov Poll, June 28, 2011. http://today.yougov.com.

To Ban or Not to Ban

Also, why are some substances banned and not others? It seems that the more effective a substance is with regard to performance—regardless of how safe it is—they seem to inevitably become a banned substance.

I am curious as to the cut off point and the benefit a supplement must provide for an athlete before it makes it to the banned substance list. Some supplements, for example creatine and beta-alanine, which have a positive effect on performance, are allowed and commonly used by professional athletes, whereas EPO [erythropoietin, a hormone]—of which there are 50 varieties regarded as safe—is completely banned.

I don't want to get into too much detail about the differences between these substances and their effects, but as the basic job of all of them is to enhance performance (albeit to different levels), where is the tipping point to when a substance is deemed to have such a positive effect on performance that it is banned?

Health shops and the performance enhancing products they sell are a massive business now throughout the world, with products promising to enhance strength, power and fitness. Basically, whatever your weakness is, there will be a product available to fix it. Why then, are these products not made illegal and placed on the banned substances list?

Is it a case that it is too difficult for WADA or the relevant sporting bodies to police? Or are the economic advantages too great to interfere with? Should we not take the gloves off and allow athletes to decide for themselves what they deem necessary to take to progress in their sport and also to avoid the confusion and often costly mistakes that occur when a substance suddenly becomes banned or unbanned?

The Harmful Effects of Drugs on Sports

In my opinion, the answer is no. Safety should always be the primary concern and if you give free rein to athletes, some don't know the concept of moderation and will do harm to themselves as a result.

The long term health effects of substances such as steroids and other known banned drugs can be detrimental and cause significant health problems down the line. As for other lesser known drugs, we simply have no idea what effect they will have on the body and what negative side effects might come about if taken on a long term basis.

Playing to the rules is paramount in any sport and cheating by taking performance enhancing drugs to gain an unfair advantage just isn't on.

You will have seen for yourself the disastrous effects that illegal drug taking has had on sports such as cycling and swimming, whereas the likes of rugby and tennis have not carried the same shame. No sport is free from drug taking but some are less affected. This may in part be due to the very regular and random drug [testing] that takes place. One of the reasons so many cyclists are found out, for example, is because it is one of the most closely monitored sports.

In sport, the grind and dedication that is required to succeed is enormous and by allowing people to accelerate or skip past certain parts of that journey is simply wrong. The respect and admiration bestowed upon any athlete is gained because of the appreciation of their hard work and the sacrifices they make.

Most people have been involved in some type of sporting activity and reached their sticking point; you've probably been there yourself. To see an athlete push through these points and to succeed where they have previously failed is what people admire and what makes sport so popular.

When you add drugs into the equation, any admiration is lost—just look at the battering the reputations of cyclist Alberto Contador or baseball player Barry Bonds have taken after being linked with performance enhancing drugs.

Drugs Undercut Sport's Challenges

When you think about what sport is all about, it revolves around the overcoming of challenges. It inspires us by appealing to our perseverance and courage. It makes us want to work that bit harder, take on new challenges and gives us the belief to overcome obstacles.

By taking performance enhancing drugs to make those challenges easier to overcome, you are ignoring what makes sport so appealing in the first place. As a result, regular testing is paramount so that all sports maintain their integrity and continue to bring life to its followers.

> ### EVALUATING THE AUTHOR'S ARGUMENTS:
>
> Johnny O'Connor believes performance-enhancing drugs undercut the admirable qualities of sports. What are those qualities, and how does he relate these to the notion of fairness?

Performance-Enhancing Drugs Do Not Ruin the Fairness of Sports

"The so-called fairness argument often pressed to justify the prohibition of performance enhancers is unable to hit its target."

Craig L. Carr

Craig L. Carr is a professor of political science at Portland State University in Oregon. He has published several books, including one titled *On Fairness*. In the following viewpoint, Carr rejects the argument that performance-enhancing drugs interfere with the fairness of competitive sports. He maintains that drug therapies are another form of athletic preparation like weight training and dieting. Drugs are not a substitute for raw talent, Carr insists, and therefore they only raise performance levels. Because human performance levels are always expanding through a variety of athletic regimens, drugs should not be discounted or singled out on the grounds of disrupting fairness.

Craig L. Carr, "Fairness and Performance Enhancement in Sports," *Journal of the Philosophy of Sport*, vol. 35, no. 2, 2008, pp. 193–207.

AS YOU READ, CONSIDER THE FOLLOWING QUESTIONS:
1. What does Carr suggest is the point and purpose of sport?
2. According to the author, what faulty notion do some critics see as a "limiting condition of athletic accomplishment"?
3. Although Carr refutes this concept, what does Michael Sandel argue sports competitions test?

Performance enhancers are not performance replacers; they do not replace the skill required, say, to hit a baseball, throw a javelin, or stop a puck. They may enhance foot speed, strength, endurance, and agility, and this almost certainly will make good athletes better. Some athletes may benefit more from steroid use than others because their bodies are better able to assimilate the drug; this is an empirical question . . . that I will not bother to speculate upon. But . . . this is likely true of any manner of preparatory activity. Some bodies may take better to carbo-loading than other bodies, for example. But this is not the only objection I wish to press. . . . We should not lose sight of the fact that the use of questionable performance enhancers does not make athletes good athletes; while it may be part of the equation, it remains only a part. Athletes must still perfect the skills, talents, and abilities tested by their sport. And these concerns still significantly affect the outcome of a given competition and may continue to determine this outcome even if it happens that A's body is better at assimilating steroids than B's body happens to be.

Athletes, Not Drugs, Win Competitions

The point, quite simply, is this: performance enhancers do not win athletic competitions; athletes do. Performance enhancers don't do much good if an athlete doesn't have much ability to enhance. With dedication and effort, performance enhancers might raise an athlete's performance level. But if the point and purpose of sport is to display excellence of the sort tested by a given sport, and if performance enhancers increase athletic ability, then dedicated athletes that use performance enhancers of any sort should raise the level of excellence in their sport. If the demonstration of such excellence is the point and purpose of play, then it would seem that fairness should at least allow their use rather than prevent it. At the competitive phase, athletes must still compete and showcase their skills in the process. If the point is excellence, it makes sense to permit athletes to engage in practice regimens, dietary caution, rigorous training techniques, and skill development drills at the preparatory phase. This is at least part of the route to excellence, but the point is to achieve excellence. And this is why it seems mistaken to regulate or control athlete activity at the preparatory phase. This, in turn, would seem to include the use of performance enhancing substances and techniques.

No Limits on Human Excellence

It may be objected, however, that these comments still do not reach the heart of the fairness objection because they continue to overlook or ignore the human component that is presumably the central focus of athletic competition. By transforming mere mortals into supermen, sport becomes a test of, say, chemistry, rather than *human* talent and ability. I have said something already intended to question this view, of course; athletes must still master the skills, abilities, and challenges posed by their chosen sport. But something more needs to be said on this score because there is something odd about supposing that some baseline notion of what a human being is lies at the heart of athletic competition. The ability of human beings to run, jump, lift great amounts of weight, swim, vault, and so forth has evidently improved over the years (if record bests are to be believed), and it has done so by virtue of the performance enhancing strategies and methods employed by athletes, trainers, and doctors. It seems strange, in light of this growth, to suppose that something like humanness is a limiting condition of athletic accomplishment. Our sense of human accomplishment is continually expanding and emerging. Chemistry has contributed to this expanding sense of what

> **FAST FACT**
>
> Though he was disqualified after testing positive for steroid use, Ben Johnson achieved a time of 9.79 seconds for the 100-meter race at the 1988 Olympics. That time has since been equaled or exceeded by five other male Olympian sprinters.

Here you can see all the Tour de France cyclists unsuspected of taking steroids.

human beings are capable of, though it is hardly alone in this regard. But chemistry has not transformed athletes into nonhuman superbeings any more than weight training has; it has merely increased human potential. The associated health costs that seem to accompany the use of some performance enhancers may hardly be worth the realized benefit, of course, but this is no part of the fairness argument. Athletic talent and ability may, and likely will, continue to grow and evolve as human beings grow and evolve, and it seems unnecessarily arbitrary to think that there is some "natural" limit to all this. Humans are progressive beings both intellectually and athletically, and while it might make some sense to worry at some point about the unhappy consequences of certain developmental techniques, these concerns seem quite foreign to the fairness argument.

Supplementing Native Abilities

There is still another way to understand the fairness argument that again suggests that certain performance enhancers are inconsistent with the point and purpose of sport. I have in mind here [Harvard philosophy professor] Michael Sandel's claim that sport is intended to test something he calls "giftedness." Sandel's argument, as I understand it, is that sport is intended to "call forth and celebrate certain talents and virtues worth admiring." Artificial methods of performance enhancement obscure this end and cheapen the excellence associated with natural talent and ability as these things are displayed through sport. As Sandel puts it, "[A]s the role of the enhancement increases, our admiration for the achievement fades.". . .

But this too seems mistaken. Great athletes are often quite gifted, of course—Sandel offers the example of the grace and elegance Joe DiMaggio displayed while patrolling center field for the New York Yankees. But I think people also admire less gifted athletes who work hard to develop whatever ability they have and get the most from modest gifts through hustle, hard work, and exceptional effort. However, even if I am wrong about this, I also think it terribly difficult to separate giftedness from effort in the case of elite athletes for the purpose of privileging one over the other. Giftedness alone is hardly sufficient, in this day, to enable athletes to achieve athletic excellence. Many extremely gifted athletes can be found sitting on barstools waiting for softball season to roll around simply because they were too lazy, too distracted, or too undisciplined to make the effort required to play center field for the Yankees or anyone else.

This response to Sandel should not be understood to indicate that I'm just switching cavalierly between emphasizing effort or ability for the sake of argument. My point, rather, is that it seems mistaken to isolate one from the other for the purpose of locating the excellence we value in sport. What we value, in my judgment, is the excellence we observe at the competitive phase of sport, and regardless of what has transpired at the preparatory phase. Once again, methods of performance enhancement make athletes stronger, faster, quicker, and more durable, and with practice and effort, this supplements their native abilities. As a result, they may perform better at the competitive phase of sport. But there is nothing in this that seems to indicate that they have defected in some way from the point or purpose of the game. To do things calculated to make one better during competition, to better display the abilities tested by the sport, seems entirely consistent with the spirit of fair play, and thus it hardly seems to qualify as unfair.

The Fairness Argument Fails

There may of course be legitimate reasons to prohibit the use of certain methods of performance enhancement. I have argued here only that the so-called fairness argument often pressed to justify the prohibition of performance enhancers is unable to hit its target. Athletes that use performance enhancing techniques that are prohibited in their sport are no doubt playing unfairly, but there is still reason to wonder why society is justified in intervening at the preparatory phase of sport in order to regulate how athletes may legitimately prepare for competition. Once we become clear on the nature of fairness as this moral virtue applies to sport, it seems we cannot justify this intervention by invoking fairness concerns alone.

EVALUATING THE AUTHOR'S ARGUMENTS:

Craig L. Carr insists that spectators admire more than just the giftedness of great athletes. He maintains that the desire to root for the underdog, the athlete who uses all means at his or her disposal—including performance-enhancing drugs—to overcome a challenge, is also part of an audience's admiration. Does this facet of Carr's argument seem like something Johnny O'Connor, the author of the previous viewpoint, overlooked? How do you think O'Connor might respond to this argument?

Performance-Enhancing Drugs Should Be Legalized in Sports If They Are Safe and Beneficial

"The use of drugs to accelerate recovery and to enhance the expression of human ability [is] a part of the spirit of sport."

Julian Savulescu

In the viewpoint that follows, Julian Savulescu claims that because of the difficulties of drug monitoring and the failure of the drug war, sports should condone the use of performance-enhancing drugs. In Savulescu's opinion, drugs that are safe and do not interfere with the spirit of a particular sport should be tolerated and regulated. As Savulescu maintains, drugs are just another means of enhancing athletic ability, a common desire among all athletes who seek to excel at their chosen profession. Savulescu is the Uehiro Chair in Practical Ethics and the director of the Centre for Practical Ethics at the University of Oxford in England.

AS YOU READ, CONSIDER THE FOLLOWING QUESTIONS:

1. According to Savulescu, how many sports face a drug problem?
2. What specific performance-enhancing drug does Savulescu claim was once illegal in sports but is now permitted because authorities have ruled it safe?
3. Why does Savulescu argue that regulated access to performance-enhancing drugs would be fairer to athletes who currently abide by the ban?

Two great sporting events are about to commence [in June 2010]: Le Tour de France and the Football [Soccer] World Cup. Doping will play a part in both of these. In every professional sport where doping could confer an advantage, there is doping. Even if it is not widespread and even if you don't know about it.

This is most obvious in Le Tour. Since it began in 1903, riders have used drugs to cope with the ordeal, resorting to alcohol, caffeine, cocaine, amphetamines, steroids, growth hormone, EPO [erythropoietin, a hormone] and blood doping. But all sports, even the World Cup, face the drug problem. The enormous rewards for the winner, the effectiveness of the drugs and the low rate of testing all create a cheating 'game' that has proved irresistible to some athletes. It is irresistible because of human nature. And the cheating athletes are now winning.

Difficulty of Drug Detection

Drugs such as EPO and growth hormone are natural chemicals in the body and are hard to detect. And the task will get tougher still. Athletes have returned to simple blood doping (having their own blood donated prior to competition and retransfused during the event), which is virtually impossible to detect if done properly. Gene doping, for example, will be equally difficult to detect. This is a technique which allows the introduction of genes into an athlete's own genetic material, or DNA, to improve muscular strength or endurance.

Also, the injection of an insulin-like growth factor (proven to increase muscle strength in mice) into the muscles of athletes would be simple. Detection would require muscle biopsy, slicing a core of

One of the world's premier sporting events is the annual Tour de France cycle race. The race has come under fire for becoming a cheating game by athletes who use various forms of performance-enhancing drugs.

muscle to examine under a microscope, which would be dangerous and difficult. EPO genes could also be directly integrated into athletes' DNA. Such gene therapy already works in monkeys.

There are only two options. We can try to ratchet up the war on doping. But this will fail, as the war on all victimless crimes involving personal advantage have failed (look at the war on alcohol, drugs and prostitution). Or we can regulate the use of performance-enhancing drugs.

Safe Drugs Are Consistent with Sport

Some performance enhancers which were once illegal, such as caffeine, have been legalised because they are safe enough. This has had no adverse effects on sport and has removed the necessity of policing a ban and the problem of cheating.

Some controversy could have been avoided if we allowed riders to take EPO or blood dope up to some safe level, for example, where their red blood cells make up 50 per cent of their blood. This level is deemed safe by the International Cycling Union and this level is easily detected by a simple, reliable and cheap blood test. Other drugs such as growth hormone can be monitored by evaluating athletes' health, looking for signs of excess, rather than trying to detect what is a normal hormone.

A rational, realistic approach to doping would be to allow safe performance-enhancing drugs which are consistent with the spirit of a particular sport, and to focus on evaluating athletes' health. Some interventions would change the nature of a sport, like creating webbed hands and feet in swimming, and should be banned on those grounds. But the use of drugs to increase endurance is a part of sport's history.

The rules of a sport are not God-given, but are primarily there for 4 reasons: (1) they define the nature of a particular display of physical excellence; (2) create conditions for fair competition; (3) protect health; (4) provide a spectacle. Any rule must be enforceable. The current zero tolerance to drugs fails on the last three grounds and is unenforceable. The rules can be changed. We can better protect the health of competitors by allowing access to safe performance-enhancement and monitoring their health. We provide a better spectacle if we give up the futile search for undetectable drugs, and focus on measurable issues relevant to the athlete's health.

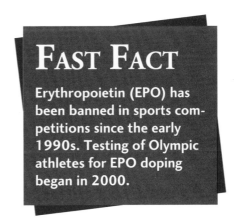

FAST FACT

Erythropoietin (EPO) has been banned in sports competitions since the early 1990s. Testing of Olympic athletes for EPO doping began in 2000.

Regulation Is Better than Prohibition

Given the pay-offs in terms of glory and money, some athletes will always access a black market of dangerous banned drugs which confer an extra advantage. But overall, regulated access is better than prohibition, as the honest athletes presently have no access to performance-enhancers.

Under a regulated market, they would have access to some safe performance-enhancers. This would narrow the advantage gap

The Benefits and Risks of Commonly Used Performance-Enhancing Drugs

Performance-Enhancing Drug	Benefits	Risks
Anabolic androgenic steroids (AAS)	Increase lean muscle mass at high doses; make users feel less fatigued; increase protein synthesis; stimulate the production of growth hormone	Acne, breast enlargement in males; shrinking of the testicles; development of male physical characteristics in females; joint problems; elevated liver enzymes; increased aggression; high blood pressure
Ephedrine	Increases energy during exercise; increases mental concentration	Cardiovascular problems; stroke
Human growth hormone (HGH)	Increases lean muscle mass and protein synthesis; decreases body fat	Insulin resistance; joint problems; pituitary gland hormone imbalance; hypertension; enlarged heart

Taken from: Marifel Mitzi F. Fernandez and Robert G. Hosey. "Performance-Enhancing Drugs Snare Nonathletes, Too." *Journal of Family Practice*, January 2009.

between the cheats and the honest athletes. And we would create a stimulus for the market to produce new, safe performance-enhancers. Limited resources could be better deployed to detect the dangerous drugs.

The World Anti-Doping Agency (WADA) claims that performance enhancement is against the spirit of sport. But caffeine does not appear to have corrupted the Olympics. Athletes already radically change their bodies through advanced, technologically-driven training regimes. Tour riders receive intravenous artificial nutrition and hydration overnight because their bodies cannot take on enough food and fluid naturally.

Ben Johnson, stripped of his 100 metres Olympic gold at the 1988 Games, said that the human body was not designed to run the speeds it is called upon to run now, and steroids were necessary to recover from the gruelling training and injuries. Jacques Anquetil, the great

French cyclist, once asked a French politician if "they expect us to ride the Tour on mineral water". Far from demonising these great athletes, we should admire them.

The use of drugs to accelerate recovery and to enhance the expression of human ability [is] a part of the spirit of sport. Some drugs, such as the modest use of EPO or growth hormone, can enhance the expression of physical excellence in sport. The challenge is to understand the spirit of each sport, and which drugs are consistent with this. But performance-enhancement per se is not against the spirit of sport; it is the spirit of sport. To choose to be better is to be human.

What is ruining sport is cheating. But cheating can be reduced by changing the rules. Cheating can be better reduced by allowing drugs rather than banning them.

EVALUATING THE AUTHOR'S ARGUMENTS:

Julian Savulescu claims that performance-enhancing drugs, when administered safely, help athletes express the capabilities of the human body and create a better spectacle for audiences. Do you agree with this opinion? Explain using evidence from this or other viewpoints in this chapter.

Performance-Enhancing Drugs Should Be Legalized in Sports to Push the Boundaries of Athleticism and Science

"By keeping [scientific] advances off the field, we're holding back possibilities."

Ryan Bradley

Some critics of performance-enhancing drugs argue that they turn sports into a contest not among athletes but among chemists. In the following viewpoint, Ryan Bradley, a senior associate editor of *Popular Science*, does not dispute this claim; he endorses it. In Bradley's opinion, athletics could, and perhaps should, be as much about human engineering as about natural talent. Drugs, according to Bradley, are just another means of pushing the limits of human performance, and that has always been part of athleticism. He advocates that a ban on performance-enhancing drugs is unjust because it keeps athletes from becoming faster and stronger and subsequently holds back scientific progress that might have other applications that all of humanity can share.

AS YOU READ, CONSIDER THE FOLLOWING QUESTIONS:
1. What argument against permitting performance enhancers in sports does Bradley say is the best argument for tolerating them?
2. Why does the author believe that regulating performance-enhancing drugs is better than outlawing them?
3. As Bradley reiterates, what was Joe Rosen's argument for advocating the continued application of science to the alteration of the human form and its capabilities?

S ports are supposed to be pure—that's why there are rules and referees; that's why the first Olympians competed in the nude. It's also the reason that the federal government is spending millions and millions of dollars investigating a famous cyclist who has, after a decade of denials and countless drug tests, returned to the center of sports scandal. It must be summer, since [seven-time Tour de France winner] Lance [Armstrong] and doping have returned to the national discussion.

It's only natural that when we discover our heroes have injected chemicals into their veins for a competitive edge (and I'm not saying Lance has, only that it's looking increasingly difficult for him to prove that he hasn't) we find them tainted and strip them of medals and put an asterisk by their names. Doping is ugly for fans but it goes beyond betrayal. Performance enhancers turn a contest between athletes into a competition among scientists and engineers. This is the best argument against enhancers. It's also the best argument for them.

A League of Superhuman Athletes

Let's pretend, for a minute, that a separate league exists. Let's call it the Asterisk League or, better, the League of Extraordinary Medicine. Drugs are legal but regulated. Athletes get educated about the risks, long term and short, of everything they introduce into—or onto—their bodies. Fans know exactly who is taking what and tracking their performance accordingly. Labs and scientists are inexorably linked to athletes' rise and fall. Chemist versus chemist doesn't sound like it would make great television, but the field would quickly advance to the point where records were broken daily and feats of crazy strength became the norm. Chemist versus chemist would become superhuman versus superhuman. Broadcasts could include expert scientists in the booth describing the limits of the human body and how these chemical enhancements get around that, or don't. The League of Extraordinary Medicine is more honest, its regulation more sensible, since outlawing drugs just does not work—we've got a forever War on Drugs to prove it. And our tests for drugs still aren't very good.

Oscar Pistorius, right, wins the 100-meter race at the 2008 Paralympic Games in Beijing, China. The viewpoint author says that medical advances like Pistorius's carbon-fiber legs and the use of performance-enhancing drugs are justified because they push the limits of human performance and knowledge.

Through this openness the league creates an environment where cutting-edge science is discussed daily, and celebrated, alongside athletic triumph. Better still: legitimizing enhancement would make the enhancements better. More drugs hit the market, more treatments become available, and this would trickle down to non-athletes. Would all this openness and advancement foster a more honest, inviting, even wholesome environment? Maybe. Creating a separate league where drugs are legal would, without a doubt, make competition safer for athletes. Matthew Herper, who has covered science and health (and, by extension, athletes and drugs) for a decade at *Forbes*, says as much [in a May 20, 2011, article].

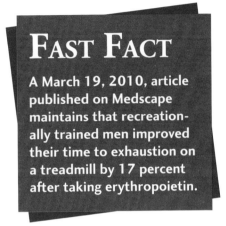

To me, the most obvious solution has always been to legalize those drugs that work, and to experimentally monitor new entrants, including dietary supplements, for both efficacy and safety. Biological improvement would be treated much as athletic equipment like baseball bats and running shoes. This could improve both athletes' performance and their health, and would be a lot better than having everybody trying whatever additive they can sneak, attempting to stay ahead of drug tests, and trusting anecdotes as a way of measuring safety and efficacy.

Holding Back Progress and Athletes

But perhaps most importantly, by keeping advances off the field, we're holding back possibilities. A few years ago I visited Hugh Herr, the director of biomechatronics at MIT's Media Lab, who had just invented a robotic ankle that would soon revolutionize prosthetics. We ended up discussing the ankle a little bit, but mostly we talked about science in sports. Herr is an athlete. As a young man he was a world-class rock climber. A week before my visit, he had been busy trying to convince the International Association of

Athletics Federations [IAAF] to allow South African runner Oscar Pistorius to compete in the Olympics. Pistorius has no legs below his knees and runs using Cheetah Flex-Foot carbon fiber limbs which, arguably, gives him an unfair advantage. Herr is also a double amputee, and walks and climbs using prosthetics. That day in his lab, while he showed me his improved ankle and described his work with veterans, Herr told me that he sees no reason why we can't make "disabled" people stronger and faster than the rest of us. In fact, we already are: just look at Pistorius. The IAAF agreed and, weeks later, decided to ban the South African from competition.

One of the best arguments for pushing, even uncomfortably, the boundaries of science and the human form was voiced by Joe Rosen, a controversial plastic surgeon. Rosen (the subject of a [July 2001] profile in *Harper's*) sees endless possibilities when the human form and science meet. But this makes people very uncomfortable. A colleague asked: "If a patient came to you and said, 'I want you to give me wings,' . . . would you actually do it?"

"Who here doesn't try to send their children to the best schools, in the hopes of altering them?" Rosen responded. "Who here objects to a Palm Pilot, a thing we clasp to our bodies, with which we receive rapid electronic signals? Who here doesn't surround themselves with a metal shell and travel at death defying speeds? We have always altered ourselves, for beauty or for power, and so long as we are not causing harm what makes us think we should stop?"

Should Performance-Enhancing Drugs in Sport Be Legalized Under Medical Supervision?

"The risks of performance enhancing drugs add to those that already exist in sport and can be completely avoided by doing without drugs all together."

Urban Wiesing

In the following viewpoint, Urban Wiesing asserts that performance-enhancing drugs should not be legalized in sports. He points out that drugs are an unnecessary addition because they may do athletes harm without conferring any advantage—especially if every athlete is given access to drugs. Furthermore, Wiesing worries that if drugs are legalized, clean athletes will feel unjustly compelled to take performance enhancers just to stay competitive. This, he argues, will ruin the perception of sports as an arena in which athletes test only their talents and training. Wiesing is the executive director of the International Centre for Ethics in the Sciences and Humanities at the University of Tuebingen in Germany.

1. As Wiesing notes, why do Karl-Heinrich Bette and Uwe Schimank claim that permitting drugs in sports would allow athletes only "free choice under pressure" in relation to the decision to take drugs or not?
2. With what notion do people associate the "spirit of sport," according to Wiesing?
3. What unfortunate message does Wiesing believe would be transmitted to young people if drugs were permitted in sports?

5. What Impact Would Legalizing Performance-Enhancing Drugs in Competitive Sport Have?

If there were a legalization of performance-enhancing drugs in competitive sports, the athletes would definitely take more risks, although, given the limits and medical supervision, the risks would be considered acceptable. The argument for legalization is usually based on the fact that athletes take risks in sport anyway, and banning doping therefore smacks of unacceptable paternalism. However, this argument fails to observe an important distinction: the risks of doping in sport are additional and avoidable, whereas other risks in sport are unavoidable. It is impossible to play football or other kinds of sport without risk of injury. Furthermore, while in many other kinds of sport the precautions taken can lower the risks, they cannot eliminate them completely. Conversely, as noted, the risks of performance-enhancing drugs add to those that already exist in sport and can be completely avoided by doing without drugs all together. However, this raises the question of whether it is beneficial to take extra, avoidable risks in sport, e.g. to make the sport more attractive, an issue that is discussed further in the next section.

Consideration of the risks of doping in sport also raises the question of whether the actions of physicians in this context would be consistent with their ethos of defining the health of the patient as their first concern. The question is raised similarly in other fields of medicine that have little to do with illness, e.g. cosmetic surgery. In these fields, it is considered acceptable to take measures that introduce a certain element of risk in order to fulfil a patient's need, even though a disease is not being treated. Again, however, a distinction needs to be made. In cosmetic surgery, some risks are unavoidable if the individual wants to improve his/her appearance through surgical intervention. In contrast, the risks involved in using performance-enhancing drugs in sport are unnecessary, which means physicians would be needlessly exposing their patients to risks in an attempt to make the sport more appealing. If physicians were administering unauthorized doping agents, they would be involved in a violation of the rules of sport.

6. The 'Gentle' Pressure to Use Performance-Enhancing Drugs

The concept of 'inherent coerciveness' would assume greater importance if limited legalization of performance-enhancing agents in sport were to come into effect. All competitive athletes have to make adjustments in many areas of their lives if they want to be successful in their given sports. Thus, the athlete has liberty to act but in the knowledge that his/her actions will have certain consequences. If the athlete were to forgo certain performance-enhancing behaviour, he/she would be less successful. The result is mentioned by Bette and Schimank: "The only liberty one has is to avoid elite sports or leave." If one allows the use of performance-enhancing drugs within certain boundaries, then all athletes who wished to be successful would have no choice but to use the substances that are allowed by the rules. They would have "free choice under pressure" in this respect. They would be forced to take actions that entail risks that are unnecessary in sport and confer no advantages upon their sport (see section 7). In this respect, a limited legalization of performance-enhancing drugs would unnecessarily put further pressure on athletes to do more risky things. Conversely, "an effective policy for eliminating performance-enhancing drug use would harm no one, except those who profit from it.". . .

8. The Meaning of Sport

If a legalization of performance-enhancing drugs became a reality, the new lottery of differences in response to performance-enhancing drugs discussed in the previous section would be combined in most cases with the ingenuity of the particular sports physician and other existing factors (natural talent, discipline, training) to determine the outcomes of athletic events. It must be reiterated at this point that a limited legalization would not exclude continued use of prohibited doping methods, perhaps in addition to use of permitted agents. It also seems likely that the more the permitted drugs were limited to minimize risks, the greater the temptation would be to use prohibited doping measures.

Crucially, a legalization of performance-enhancing drugs would have a massive impact on our perception of sport. It would ultimately compromise the current, widely accepted 'spirit of sport'. Sport is an artificial setting, created by human beings, in which the competitor is required to perform, at least according to current, widely prevalent belief, with a degree of 'naturalness'. The sports-watching audience is interested in "athletic performance . . . not . . . biochemistry." We associate the 'spirit of sport' with the notion that achievements come

> **FAST FACT**
>
> Under World Anti-Doping Agency regulations, the penalty for violating performance-enhancing substance restrictions is a two-year suspension for first-time offenders (a four-year or greater suspension for trafficking in illicit substances or administering them to others). Multiple offences draw longer suspension periods.

through hard work, discipline, training and natural talents, even when we do not recognize this in other areas of our lives. As has been recently noted, "The fascination of sports mainly comes from the demonstration of what people are able to do on their own. Doping destroys this fascination." This culture of 'naturalness', to some extent at least, has previously been accepted as part of sport.

These ideas have given rise to highly controversial discussions on what the 'meaning of sport' is, what is meant by the 'spirit of sport' and how important this is, and whether this 'spirit of sport' is immutable. Is the 'spirit of sport' a "key constitutional quality" of sport, one that may never change or undergo 'correction', if necessary? Is doping "incompatible with the meaning of sports" or could it be considered consistent with the 'spirit of sport'? For example, it has been suggested in a recent publication that "Performance-enhancement [. . .] embodies the spirit of human sport."

Unfortunately, these questions cannot be answered at this point. It is not possible to determine what exactly constitutes the 'spirit of sport' and whether our views on this should change. However, and this is the central argument of this article, it is not necessary to settle these questions because a limited legalization of drugs in sports and the consequent change in the current perception of the 'spirit of sport' would have no advantages. Any other concept of the 'spirit of sport' should have to be proven to be advantageous in itself, and such advantages cannot be identified. There is no need to ponder whether the 'spirit of sport' is or should be subject to change because there is simply no good reason to make any such change in any case.

However, it is important to clarify three aspects of 'naturalness of performance' in sport. The first is the difficulty of determining what constitutes a 'natural' measure of improving performance. Many permissible training methods and food supplements are in some ways less 'natural' than other things that athletes may do. However, the fact that defining an acceptable limit for such measures, particularly when the dividing line appears to be opinion-based and is established on a more or less continuous spectrum, does not necessarily mean that we should dispense with such limits. Furthermore, this is not the approach taken in other areas of life. The difficulties inherent in putting forward arguments as to why one substance or another should or should not be on the World Anti-Doping Agency list are not sufficient reasons to characterize their list as completely arbitrary and, therefore, irrelevant.

Second, it must be clearly stated that 'naturalness' in sport is not considered as a value in itself, but only as a value in this specific context. In sport, great importance is attached to the 'naturalness' of achievements, whereas in other areas of life this is not necessarily the case. Thus, there is no requirement in this context to argue that 'naturalness' is a value in itself.

Third, according special attention and value on 'naturalness' of performance in sport means that sport is considered different to other areas of life, in which certain 'artificial' measures of obtaining improvement are allowed. A "premature (adjustment)" to this aspect of sport threatens destruction of the uniqueness of sport. Sport would no longer be a "special area," a "counter-world of 'personal achievement.'"

9. The Exemplary Role of Sport
Another argument for the need to protect the 'spirit of sport' can be put forward. There can be no doubt that sport, playful in nature, but still in

accordance with the rules, sets an example for society. As Albert Camus once said, "After many years during which I saw many things, what I know most surely about morality and the duty of man I owe to sport." Sport shows, with its rules and requirement for fairness, how to deal with other problems in society. It conveys an attitude that acts as a role model in many other areas of human life and . . . "in a sense, it can be a model for a better society." The question then is: how would legalization of performance-enhancing drugs affect the exemplary character of sport?

On this issue, three different facets of the functions of role models need to be distinguished. An aspect of society can take on the function of a role model if it (i) sets special, exemplary standards; (ii) respects certain standards in a special and exemplary way; or (iii) controls or ensures compliance with the standards in an exemplary way.

First, it is useful to consider the ongoing impact of sports as a role model in these three areas if the ban on performance-enhancing drugs remained in place as follows:

- With respect to setting standards, sport would remain a model at least for most citizens.
- Continued violations of the norm (standard) would be anticipated and the function of sport as a role model in terms of respecting standards in a special and exemplary way would continue to be debatable.
- The system of controlling or ensuring compliance with standards in sport is currently unconvincing, with many doping violations remaining undiscovered. Improving the control system would depend on further technical developments (e.g. in the collation of indirect evidence), which would make the system more convincing and therefore more able to act as a role model.

Second, it is important to consider how the exemplary role of sport could change if doping were legalized as follows:

- At least for a significant part of society, sport would lose its function as a role model because the model standard it exemplifies would be abolished.
- With a limited legalization of performance-enhancing agents, continued violations of the new norm would be anticipated because the potential for the use of additional banned but performance-enhancing substances would remain. In terms of the exemplary role of strict adherence to standards, nothing would be gained from legalizing the use of performance-enhancing agents.

- The cost of control would remain unchanged and the suspicion that the control system was not effective would remain. Again, therefore, nothing would be gained in these respects compared with the existing ban. The function of the role model would also still be dependent on further technical development.

To summarize, a legalization of performance-enhancing drugs would definitely result in some lessening of the exemplary role of sport in terms of setting standards. The same challenges that exist at present would need to be faced with respect to the other facets of role model function. Overall, the function of sport as a role model would be reduced.

10. Children and Adolescents and the Legalization of Performance-Enhancing Drugs

As discussed in the previous section, a legalization of performance-enhancing drugs would diminish the function of sport as a role model, and this would particularly be the case with respect to children and adolescents. Self-restraint would be abandoned and the message would be that one must be willing to do anything for success. This 'boundless willingness' is not a preferred role model, especially for youth. As stated in a recent publication on doping in sport: "Also of concern is the will expressed when one takes performance enhancers [. . .] to force a specific peak output with all available means. It is doubtful whether one should raise children according to a life plan which links life satisfaction to the boundless willingness to provide peak performance."

Moreover, the consequences would be devastating for children and adolescents who are directly affected, i.e. training for a career as an athlete. A total ban on doping for children and adolescents when there is simultaneous legalization for adults is impracticable and would not seem to be feasible. Also, the manner in which children and adolescents under the age of 18 years (which is an advanced age in many sports) react to performance enhancers is not known. However, supporters of a legalization of performance-enhancing drugs do not exclude children and adolescents. Rather, they justify approval of doping in these age groups by pointing out that competitors at this stage are taking various risks in sports anyway: "[. . .] if children are allowed

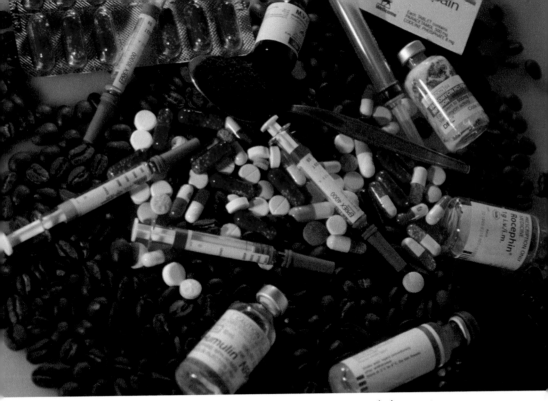

Proponents of banning performance-enhancing drugs in sports say such drug use is not desirable because it is coercive, can cause significant harm, and advances no social values.

to train as professional athletes, then they should be allowed to take the same drugs, provided that they are no more dangerous than their training is."

Why is this reasoning not convincing? First, the long-term consequences of even supposedly harmless drugs in children and adolescents cannot be determined on the basis of available evidence. It is irresponsibly optimistic to believe that powerful biological interventions during childhood and adolescence do not have unwanted side effects over the longer term. Second, Savulescu et al. again do not distinguish between unavoidable risks and additional, avoidable risks. The fact is that professional sports training for children and adolescents entails risks to both their health and their psychosocial development. These can be partly avoided (and should be avoided), but are not completely avoidable. However, this does not mean that further avoidable risks for children and adolescents therefore need not be avoided! Trying to justify an additional, avoidable (and senseless) evil by pointing out the existence of another, unavoidable evil is not a persuasive argument. The only reasonable course of action for people who are concerned about the welfare of children and who wish to preserve the "educational credibility" of sport is to ensure that unavoidable risks are minimized as much as possible and avoid the clearly avoidable risks associated with professional sports training for children. The latter includes the risks associated with doping.

11. Conclusions

The arguments for and against the legalization of performance-enhancing drugs in sport operate on two different levels. On one level, there are pragmatic arguments concerned with the effort required to establish and enforce controls, the quality and quantity of these controls, and the responsibility for and costs of regulations. Also on this level are arguments concerning the need to preserve the audience's trust in sport, freedom of choice for athletes, the justification for introducing additional risks and the need to avoid risk, especially in children and adolescents. On another level, there are also arguments that touch on the 'spirit of sport' and the 'naturalness' of performance in sport. Whether this 'spirit of sport' has a "central constitutional quality" which one may not change under any circumstances, or whether in fact it can be modified, remain as controversial as the question of whether doping is consistent with the true 'spirit of sport' or not. However, these disputes do not have to be resolved in order to answer the question of whether drugs should be legalized under medical supervision. Even if it were thought acceptable to abolish normative behavior consistent with the 'spirit of sport' and that it would be then still possible to perform with a degree of 'naturalness', this step should be taken only if advantages could be expected to ensue. However, this is not the case at all; a legalization of performance-enhancing drugs would confer no advantages and therefore would make no sense. The natural lottery of athletic talent would be only partially compensated for, and would also be complemented by, the natural lottery of responsiveness to doping measures combined with the inventiveness of doping doctors. There would be no gains in terms of 'justice' for athletes from legalizing doping; at best, the benefits of doping misconduct would be reduced in the case of limited legalization, but a performance advantage from using non-permitted drugs could still be obtained. This is important, because in professional sport, even small advantages can be decisive. Doping also entails avoidable risks that are not necessary to increase the attractiveness of the sport. Furthermore, many risks, particularly over the long term, are difficult to anticipate. Legalization would not reduce the restrictions on athletes' freedom; the control effort would remain the same, if not increased. Extremely complicated international regulations would have to be adopted. Athletes, including children and adolescents involved in competitive sport, would be forced to take additional, avoidable health risks. Audience mistrust, particularly in regard to athletes who had achieved outstanding feats, would remain because these athletes could still be relying upon the use of illegal practices. The all-time best lists would remain unreliable. The game of 'tortoise and the hare' between doping athletes and inspectors would continue because prohibited but not identifiable practices could provide additional benefits with respect to the use of permissible drugs. Above all, the function of sport as a role model would clearly be damaged.

The legalization of drugs in sport is not desirable because it is "coercive, has significant potential for harm, and advances no social value." Nothing would be gained, but a lot would be lost. The 'spirit of sport', exhibited in an artificial setting where performance with a certain degree of 'naturalness' is expected, would be abandoned without gain. These considerations suggest that the legalization of performance-enhancing drugs in sport, even under medical supervision, should not be entertained.

EVALUATING THE AUTHOR'S ARGUMENTS:

In making his argument against the legalization of drugs in athletic competitions, Urban Wiesing insists that performance-enhancing drugs defy the "spirit of sport." How does Wiesing define the spirit of sport? In a previous viewpoint, Julian Savulescu claims that allowing performance-enhancing drugs would benefit, not harm, sports. Do Wiesing's and Savulescu's definitions of the spirit of sport conflict? Explain why or why not, and if you believe their definitions do conflict, explain what parts of their arguments are opposed.

The Use of Human Growth Hormone Can Benefit Athletes

"When you understand what [human growth hormone] can do for athletes, and understand the nature of risks involved with playing professional sports . . . the case can be made that some supplementation may be appropriate and even necessary."

Sal V. Marinello

Sal Marinello explains in the viewpoint that follows why human growth hormone (HGH) is a desirable drug for athletes. Marinello asserts that HGH's chief benefit is that it builds and retains muscle mass. Marinello points out that HGH works at low dosages, so there is a low risk of abuse by athletes. For these reasons, Marinello believes HGH is a beneficial treatment for athletes seeking greater strength as well as injured performers who want to rebuild torn muscle. Marinello is a personal trainer and high school conditioning coach with experience writing about health and fitness for various websites.

AS YOU READ, CONSIDER THE FOLLOWING QUESTIONS:
1. According to Marinello, what is hyperplasia?
2. How is HGH used in rehabilitation therapies, as described by the author?
3. Why does Marinello claim that HGH, administered at normal doses, may be administered to normalize hormonal levels?

Here is a list of reasons as to why HGH [human growth hormone]—right now—is the ideal drug for athletes. With the latest edition of the steroids in sport scandal that involves professional athletes from Major League Baseball, as well as other sports, people need to understand why these supplements are desirable to pro athletes. And you won't get this kind of info if you depend on the mainstream media and sports news outlets. . . .

Body builders have enjoyed the benefits of human growth hormone, used in conjunction with a variety of other anabolic agents, for over 20 years but only in recent years have legit athletes started to catch on to this "better" kind of performance enhancing drugs.

HGH Builds Muscle

1) Human growth hormone provides a potent anabolic effect; it builds muscle. Without turning this into a biochem lesson—especially since that's way over my head—suffice to say that HGH increases the body's ability to synthesize protein, and that this allows for muscle tissue to be built. Human growth hormone use produces the holy grail of all anabolic benefits, *hyperplasia*. Hyperplasia is the permanent increase in the amount of muscle cells. Over the years there have been many steroids that were alleged to result in creating new muscle cells, but HGH is the substance that actually delivers this incredible benefit. HGH also increases the size of existing muscle cells.

So with HGH you have a situation where the size of existing muscle cells are increased AND a permanent creation of new muscle cells. So a person could go on a cycle of human growth hormone therapy, which would create new muscle cells that remain after HGH therapy stops. The longer the person remains on this regimen the more *new* muscle cells will be produced. This person would then have more muscle than he did before the therapy and reap all of the performance benefits that come with increased muscle even after the end of therapy.

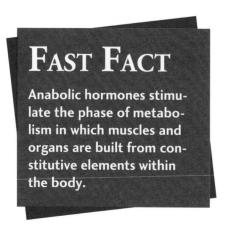

Additionally, human growth hormone has a positive strengthening effect on connective tissues such as ligaments, tendons and cartilage and at an accelerated rate. Old injuries will heal and these tissues will be strengthened, which can potentially minimize future injuries as well. There is no doubt that human growth hormone therapy is being used in conjunction with the surgery and rehab of professional athletes, which has had the effect of getting athletes back on the field quicker than ever. These connective tissue benefits make HGH much more attractive than the use of old school steroids, as steroids only positively affect muscle tissue, while having a negative effect on connective tissue.

Preserving Muscle While Burning Fat

2) HGH provides metabolic benefits such as helping the body burn more fat than usual, and serves as a protein-sparing agent as well. HGH administration triggers the release of fatty acids from fat stores and the body winds up burning more fat than carbohydrates to meet energy requirements. This is why athletes on human growth hormone can have extremely low levels of body fat while maintaining extremely high levels of muscle mass.

Without drugs, there is a kind of equilibrium between body fat and muscle mass. If body fat is too low a person's muscle mass will decrease as well. HGH also has an anti-catabolic effect (protein sparing), which means that muscle protein isn't broken down during periods of intense exercise or in the case of calorie restriction. This anti-catabolic effect means that athletes can recovery quicker from competition and training.

Low Dosage, Low Risk

3) HGH is legal and can be acquired and administered by a physician, and as a result, the intelligent athlete can use medical privacy regulations to avoid the spotlight. The dose at which HGH is effective is small, which minimizes risk and—in most cases—allows the physician to avoid breaking any laws or breaching any ethical standards.

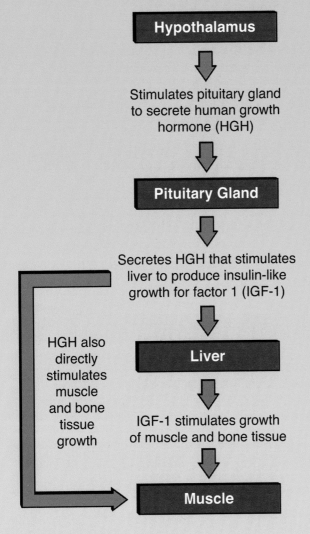

Normal Pathway of Growth Hormone Secretion

Hypothalamus

Stimulates pituitary gland to secrete human growth hormone (HGH)

Pituitary Gland

Secretes HGH that stimulates liver to produce insulin-like growth for factor 1 (IGF-1)

HGH also directly stimulates muscle and bone tissue growth

Liver

IGF-1 stimulates growth of muscle and bone tissue

Muscle

Compiled by editor.

Additionally, due to the stresses of professional sports there is a very good chance that most—if not all—athletes would test for low hormonal levels during their season. This means HGH can be administered in order to normalize an athlete's levels. This kind of therapeutic dose can provide enormous benefits to an athlete during their season. This is an important distinction to make. If an athlete does test for low HGH levels—which most would or could—this is a case of using HGH as it is intended and not abusing it.

There are doctors all across the country that are openly practicing this kind of medicine. One could argue that these doctors are incorrect in their uses of HGH, but this argument doesn't seem to hold any more weight than the counter argument that there are no appropriate "off-label" uses of HGH. These are the major reasons as to why HGH is so popular among athletes.

Understanding the Benefits

There are other reasons as well, but this is enough for now. And it is worth noting that testosterone when used in similarly appropriate doses, in conjunction with HGH is an extremely potent supplement cocktail from which all athletes would benefit greatly.

Remember, this isn't an effort to rationalize or justify the use of HGH and testosterone. I am simply recognizing and pointing out reasons why athletes—or anybody who works out for that matter—would find these substances so desirable. What I will say is that when you understand what these drugs can do for athletes, and understand the nature of risks involved with playing professional sports—especially football—the case can be made that some supplementation may be appropriate and even necessary.

EVALUATING THE AUTHOR'S ARGUMENTS:

Early in Marinello's defense of the desirability of human growth hormone among athletes, he states that "you won't get this kind of info if you depend on the mainstream media and sports news outlets." Why do you believe he adds this opinion to his main argument?

The Use of Human Growth Hormone Poses a Health Threat to Athletes

"Athletes who continue to abuse high doses of GH over long periods of time are risking detrimental effects to their health."

Nishan Guha, Peter H. Sönksen, and Richard I.G. Holt

In the following viewpoint, Nishan Guha, Peter H. Sönksen, and Richard I.G. Holt report that athletes are drawn to the use of human growth hormone (HGH) to build muscle and recover from muscle-related injuries. Despite these perceived benefits, the prolonged use of human growth hormone may have negative consequences, the authors contend. Although the long-term effects of HGH use are not documented, Guha and his colleagues believe athletes using the hormone may develop high blood pressure, liver-related problems, and heart ailments. The authors worry that HGH abuse may be widespread and that existing drug-detection methods—which are limited in their effectiveness—may not deter athletes from overusing the hormone. Guha is a clinical research fellow in

Nishan Guha, Peter H. Sönksen, and Richard I. G. Holt, "Growth Hormone Abuse: A Threat to Elite Sport," *Biologist*, vol. 57, no. 4, December, 2010, pp. 185–191. All rights reserved. Reproduced by permission.

endocrinology and metabolism at Southampton General Hospital in England. Sönksen and Holt are professors of endocrinology at the University of Southampton.

AS YOU READ, CONSIDER THE FOLLOWING QUESTIONS:

1. According to Guha and colleagues, in what publication was HGH first touted as a beneficial performance enhancer?
2. What is the most notable substance that athletes commonly abuse HGH in combination with, as stated by the authors?
3. What is acromegaly, as the authors define it?

The use of performance-enhancing substances in the sporting arena is a major threat to the health of elite athletes and to the fairness of competition. But these athletes possess a strong desire to win at all costs, as was famously illustrated in a 1995 survey of American athletes.

198 elite athletes were asked if they would use a banned performance-enhancing substance under two different scenarios. 195 athletes said yes if the scenario was 'you will not be caught and you will win'. Even when the scenario was 'you will not be caught and you will win every competition you enter for the next 5 years and then you will die from the side-effects of the substance,' more than half of the athletes still said yes.

> **FAST FACT**
>
> To outwit HGH detection methods, scientists are looking to gene therapy as a means of introducing genes into athletes' bodies to stimulate an increase in the natural production of growth hormone.

Growth hormone (GH) was first publicly advocated as a performance-enhancing agent in *The Underground Steroid Handbook* published in 1982. The author, Dan Duchaine, described the potential beneficial effects on athletic performance of anabolic steroids and other substances, including growth hormone. It was clear that GH was already being abused by bodybuilders and other athletes at this time. In fact, athletes had discovered the performance-enhancing actions of growth hormone by experimenting on themselves, long before scientists designed randomised controlled trials to test the effects of GH in adults with GH deficiency. . . .

Risks of Growth Hormone Abuse

The benefits of GH for the elite athlete have been a source of considerable debate. The potential benefits are most evident from studies in adults with GH deficiency. GH replacement results in improved exercise capacity and maximum oxygen uptake, increased muscle strength and improved body composition with decreased percentage of body fat and increased lean body mass. All of these effects have the potential to benefit performance if reproduced in healthy athletes.

For many years however, there was no randomised controlled trial evidence to demonstrate the performance-enhancing effects of GH on healthy individuals. Athletes pay little attention to evidences from clinical trials that are designed to look for relatively large, statistically significant differences between groups of participants. An athlete is seeking any small performance gain that gives them the edge over their competitors. Furthermore, athletes are known to abuse GH in

Abusing HGH may lead to symptoms similar to acromegaly (evidenced here in this overgrown hand), a disease most often associated with excess growth hormone secretion by the pituitary gland over a long period of time.

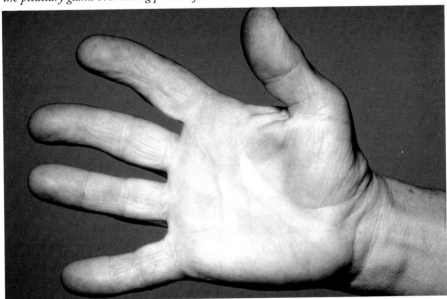

The Common Side Effects of Human Growth Hormone Use

The World Anti-Doping Agency has noted that abuse of human growth hormone may lead to:

- Diabetes in prone individuals
- Worsening of cardiovascular diseases
- Muscle, joint, and bone pain
- Hypertension and cardiac deficiency
- Abnormal growth of organs
- Accelerated osteoarthritis
- Metabolic dysfunction, including glucose intolerance and other side effects associated with excess levels of IGF-1 (produced through stimulation of the liver)

Compiled by editor.

combination with a variety of other substances, most notably anabolic steroids, whereas clinical trials are usually designed to investigate the impact of a single intervention whilst all other variables are kept constant. Some recent studies have shown improvements in physical performance in response to GH administration, and have suggested that benefits are most likely to be seen when GH is combined with other anabolic agents. The authors of one of these studies speculated that the observed increase in sprint capacity could translate to an improvement of 0.4 seconds over a 100 meter race.

The long-term adverse effects of high doses of GH are unknown but these may mimic some of the features of acromegaly, a condition characterized by excess GH secretion over a very long period of time, most often from a pituitary gland tumour. This disease may be associated with fluid retention, hypertension, insulin-resistance and an increased risk of diabetes in susceptible individuals. Other adverse features of acromegaly may include cardiomyopathy and characteristic changes in facial appearance. It has been reported, however, that the early stages of acromegaly are associated with an increase in strength and improved physical performance before the complications occur after prolonged exposure to massive GH excess.

Detection of GH Abuse

The International Olympic Committee placed GH on their list of banned substance[s] in 1989 but the detection of GH abuse has posed many challenges. Unlike many synthetic anabolic steroids, GH is a naturally occurring substance. As a result, the accusation of doping with GH must be based on finding abnormally high GH concentrations in the circulation, which cannot be explained by an underlying pathological condition such as acromegaly. In addition, GH is secreted in a pulsatile manner and random elevated GH measurements may reflect a spontaneous peak. Furthermore, a blood sample is required for GH testing rather than the conventional urine samples used for detecting anabolic steroid abuse. This is because the urinary concentration of GH is extremely low and also because the urinary excretions of GH is increased by exercise and thus urinary GH concentration is not a constant function of plasma GH concentration. This is less of an issue now that blood testing is being used in the anti-doping field in the detection of abuse with [the hormone] erythropoietin (EPO) and to detect blood doping where blood transfusions are used to increase the oxygen-carrying capacity of the athlete's blood. . . .

Growth hormone remains an important challenge to anti-doping authorities despite the fact that as performance-enhancing properties remain controversial. Athletes who continue to abuse high doses of GH over long periods of time are risking detrimental effects to their health.

EVALUATING THE AUTHOR'S ARGUMENTS:

What kinds of evidence do the authors use to make their claim that human growth hormone use in sports should still be monitored by authorities? How is this argument different from Sal Marinello's defense of HGH's desirability among athletes in the previous viewpoint? Whose opinion do you find more convincing? Explain why.

Chapter 2

How Should Drug Testing Be Addressed for Professional Athletes?

Many think that sports authorities refuse to improve their drug testing methods and that new testing procedures must be implemented and abusers punished.

Viewpoint 1

Steroids in High Schools? Let's Invest in Testing

"The pros are developing progressively stricter punishment for steroid use—including banishment from the sport, and all that means in terms of money and careers."

Santa Fe New Mexican

The *Santa Fe New Mexican* is a daily newspaper published in Santa Fe, New Mexico. In the following viewpoint, the editorial's authors discuss the lack of drug testing present in high school sports. Collegiate and professional athletes are grown at the high school level, and the authors believe drug testing needs to be present in the early stages in order to deter the use of steroids later on in an athlete's career. This editorial argues that drug testing is an investment that could save lives.

AS YOU READ, CONSIDER THE FOLLOWING QUESTIONS:

1. According to the article, what percent of high school athletes are willing to take drugs and steroids in order to gain an advantage?
2. What are some cons to using steroids, as stated in the article?
3. Do the authors believe that drug testing would deter student athletes from using steroids?

So does that hot-shot high-school halfback owe his blazing speed and mountainous muscles only to endless hours of weight training and workouts? Or has he been doing the same as some of his role models—taking steroids?

The professional sports leagues are finally admitting that a certain number of their star players are creations of chemistry, and scurrying to impose more serious sanctions on the shooter-uppers before Congress comes up with really heavy ones.

Both the pros and our nation's collegiate athletic factories perform random testing for performance-enhancing drugs. But at the high-school level, where professional athletes are grown, there's been strong denial that steroids are a problem—at least not such a severe problem that mandatory testing has been imposed.

But a recent study, commissioned by the National Institute on Drug Abuse, shows plenty of high-schoolers—perhaps 6 or 7 percent—willing to gamble their health, even their lives, on drugs that'll give 'em an unfair advantage over kids competing for a spot on the team, or athletes from other schools.

FAST FACT

According to a March 2005 ABC News/ESPN poll, only 18 percent of Americans agreed that Major League Baseball authorities are doing enough to prevent steroid use in their sport.

You'd think that, being in school, they'd be educated about the stupidity of pumping up on mind-altering, body-deteriorating drugs. Or that their coaches, delighted as they might be over the idea of bulked-up ballcarriers and beefy linemen, would earnestly warn their charges—not only of the long-term health dangers of steroids, but also of what happens when they're caught.

The pros are developing progressively stricter punishment for steroid use—including banishment from the sport, and all that means in terms of money and careers. Colleges, too, have come up with sanctions.

And it's time, says Gov. Bill Richardson, for New Mexico high schools to begin random testing for steroids. He's calling for a $330,000 pilot program, to begin next summer.

He acknowledges a lack of data on steroids in our state—but notes that ignorance is anything but bliss: "We may be talking about a drug problem that is out of control and we don't know it," he said this week at a conference that included high school athletics leaders and officials from the federal Drug Enforcement Administration.

It's an investment that could save lives—not only those of the steroid consumers, who open themselves to heart disease, liver and kidney trouble, testicular atrophy and other awfulness, but also those of the skinny kids lining up against these artificial behemoths.

Maybe steroids aren't the problem here in Santa Fe that they are in other places, as some coaches and athletes told *The New Mexican*'s John Sena. Indeed, our community's kids tend to be lithe basketball players, not the kind of earth-shaking beasts seen on Sunday TV.

All the same, they guessed that at least a few of our state's athletes use the stuff. And we'd guess that the threat of random testing would deter a fair number of aspiring collegiate and professional athletes.

Such tests shouldn't have to go on forever; now that the dirty secret of steroid use no longer is a secret, and now that the big boys are acting on that guilty knowledge, the country is likely to see an end to it—at least until someone comes up with an undetectable form of it.

Beyond testing, there's got to be clear warning of steroid dangers—and public condemnation of the stuff as out-and-out cheating.

EVALUATING THE AUTHOR'S ARGUMENTS:

The *Santa Fe New Mexican* argues that random drug testing of athletes would deter the use of steroids. Is the article convincing in its argument?

Viewpoint

2

Drug Testing in Sports Is Suspect and Should Be Reconsidered

Anthony P. Millar

"There is nothing to suggest that doping will ever be eliminated. There has been no effort made to clean up the area that would inspire confidence."

In the following viewpoint, Anthony P. Millar claims that the current practice of testing athletes for drugs is poorly conceived. In Millar's opinion, arguments for drug testing in the name of fairness and the possible loss of fans are faulty and should not impact drug-banning policy. In addition, he asserts that the rules for banning specific drugs are arbitrary and difficult to enforce. Because of these flaws, as well as the burden of proof placed on athletes who are accused of drug-taking, Millar advocates a rethinking of drug policies, stating that the best short-term solution is to accept that drugs will play a part in sports and provide the best medical advice to athletes to reduce the potential harms from abuse. Millar is the director of research at the Lewisham Sports Medicine Institute in Australia.

Drug testing was introduced at the Grenoble Winter Games in 1968 and since then it has been pursued under a "law and order" approach. As there are still positives being found, it is obvious that drug use has not been eliminated. Information about the number of tests performed and the frequency of positives is not readily available from all sporting bodies and, even if they were accessible, previous experience would make one wary of accepting them. There are no independent examiners to allay any doubts. As drug testing is expensive and penalties are not uniform, it is time . . . that the whole program was reassessed. Under the present system athletes bear the total punishment and personal denigration but similar treatment must also be handed out to the judges in competitions who cheat, to officials of associations who sweep positives under the table and members of medical commissions who connive to free positive testing athletes. Those who manage the athletes and help them to contravene the rules also deserve to share the same punishment as the athlete. This includes the trainers, physicians, coaches and others who promulgate the values of drug taking and encourage athletes to break the law. . . .

Two Main Reasons to Ban Drugs

The reasons for banning the use of Performance Enhancing Substances (PES) fall into two main areas. The use of the substance is unfair and, when that fails, there is a danger to the athlete that needs to be considered. These two categories encompass the arguments of opponents of the use of PES and need to be addressed if there is to be a system that is equitable to everyone. A further argument is that sponsors will be deterred if drugs are used in high level sport and that governments will act adversely and withdraw support. There is nothing to support this thesis. Fans come to see Herculean efforts and the fact that competitors may have used drugs has not deterred record attendances. The fans want to be entertained and the popularly held belief that all athletes take drugs has not deterred attendees.

Dismissing the Fairness Objection

The concept of fairness suggests all are equal. The obvious genetic variations between participants show how unfair the system can be. A consideration of the variation in height in competitors in the high jump shows the impossibility of a man 160 cms [centimeters, about 5 feet 2 inches] winning the high jump. This is accepted as innate but it is still unfair to the short athlete. In boxing, weight categories lessen the differences and are fairer to the lighter boxer. This could be done in athletics but there is no interest on the part of organisers to level the playing field to diminish the stress of unfairness. Social factors intrude into training. Some athletes are supported by the state or a foundation giving them an advantage over the competitor who has to work to supply family needs and is thus restricted in the time available to train and cannot afford overseas competition. There is an unequal availability of Sports Medicine support between countries. Specialised equipment is more accessible in affluent countries. These differences show that a level playing field is an impossibility. . . . It is incongruous that drugs are the only item equally available to all sporting participants. The fact that one athlete may not want to take them should not affect another. If an athlete only wishes to train two days a week, this should not restrict his opponents. He must be prepared to come last. And a similar approach could apply to drugs.

No Proven Health Risks

When the appeal to fairness fails, the next target is the danger to health from drug use. The main drugs attacked are the anabolic steroids. They have been credited with causing heart disease, but there has been no follow up of former users to confirm the excessive occurrence of heart disease in users. Studies have shown there is no difference in left ventricular measurements between users and non-users. More recent studies have shown that the changes in the ventricular wall persist for an

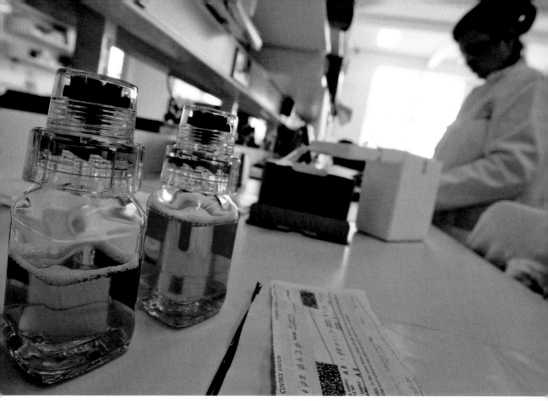

A laboratory technician processes athletes' urine samples in Great Britain as part of the program formed by the World Anti-Doping Agency and the International Olympic Committee in an attempt to control or limit doping in sports.

extended period in a gradually diminishing way. Later studies showed that the abnormality in left ventricular hypertrophy decreased over the years, suggesting that eventually the changes may not be detectable. Changes in lipid profiles have been reported, but the changes reverted to normal after the course of steroids was completed. There is no evidence to support the view that a reduction in HDL [high density lipoprotein] for 3 or even 6 months has any significant effect on coronary artery disease. When one considers users do not smoke, eat low fat diets and train regularly, all recommended actions to minimise heart disease, there is a need for further investigation to evaluate the long-term effects of steroids and any supposed link to heart disease. . . .

Human Growth Hormone is a newer addition to the pharmaceutical armoury and reports are less frequent about its adverse effects. Most are based on the idea that any problem is likely to be a variation of acromegaly. There have been sporadic reports of skin changes and organ enlargement but little of a documented thesis which can be evaluated. Erythropoietin has been shown to increase blood viscosity and this is deleterious to performance. Other substances used such as ephedrine and caffeine have even worse documentation when their effect on performance is assessed. There is a great need for further research into such substances if advice is to be given to the athletes and their testers.

Fan Base Is Not Likely to Decrease

It is difficult to believe that the TV firms who pay such exorbitant amounts of money to televise high level sport would be worried, in private at least, that some or all athletes were using drugs. When one recalls the days of amateurs, as distinct from professionals, receiving money under the lap, journalistic sources still reported events and the monetary rewards were considered as a just reward in spite of recriminations that sponsorship and government approval will be lost. The "crime" did not affect any programs and now all athletes are in one category and monetary gains are part of daily sport. Similarly governments accepted the state of affairs as to do otherwise would lose votes. Fans come to the events to see record breaking performances that often result from the use of drugs. The fans want to see new world records and they want to be entertained. It is common to hear today that all athletes are on drugs and there is nothing to show that it diminishes attendances or TV audiences. . . .

FAST FACT

According to a June 1, 2010, CBS News article, drug tests generally produce false-positive results in 5 to 10 percent of cases and false negatives in 10 to 15 percent of cases.

Conflicts of Interest and Arbitrary Criteria

To attempt to control or limit doping in sport, the IOC [International Olympic Committee], together with governments, formed the World Anti Doping Agency (WADA) and these two groups financed the venture. The management was vested in a former vice president of the IOC. This is a drawback as the IOC has been so tainted by corruption that any person allied with it will always be viewed with suspicion. It is interesting to reflect how a representative who raises money one day and doubtless minimises the drug problem, can a day later be pursuing drug users. Using people in roles which appear to be directly opposed to each other raises suspicions of a conflict of interest and questions the intent of the individual and the employers.

Furthermore, WADA has a number of problem areas. The criteria for including a drug on the list are open to criticism. The first criterion is that the drug improves performance or has the potential to do

The World Anti-Doping Agency's 11 Stages of Doping Control

Stage	Description
1. Athlete selection	You can be selected for doping control at any time and any place.
2. Notification	A Doping Control Officer (DCO) or chaperone will notify you of your selection and outline your rights and responsibilities.
3. Reporting to the doping control station	You should report for testing immediately. The DCO may allow you to delay reporting—however only in certain circumstances.
4. Sample collection equipment	You are given a choice of individually sealed collection equipment.
5. Your sample	You will be asked to provide a sample witnessed by a DCO or chaperone. You may additionally be asked to provide a blood sample.
6. Volume of urine	A minimum 90mL (milliliters) is required for all samples.
7. Splitting the sample	Your sample will be split into an A and B bottle.
8. Sealing the samples	You will seal the A and B bottles in accordance with the DCO's instructions.
9. Measuring specific gravity	The DCO will measure the specific gravity of the sample to ensure it is not too diluted to analyze.
10. Completing your doping control form	You have the right to provide comments regarding the conduct of your doping control session. Be sure to confirm that all of the information is correct, including the sample code number. You will receive a copy of the doping control form.
11. The laboratory process	All samples are sent to WADA-accredited laboratories.

so. Drugs have placebo effects so that any chemical has the potential to improve someone's performance and thus make it unavailable for other athletes. One has only to read the literature about food supplements to realise that taking these is an offence. Several amino acids have been shown to augment performance by stimulating the production of Growth Hormone. Will this lead to banning the foods containing the amino acid? The second criterion is that the substance may damage the athlete's health. There are not many substances that cannot damage an athlete's health when improperly used, either as a result of overdosing or an allergic response. This criterion virtually places every substance on the banned list. Even water! The third criterion is any substance that violates the spirit of sport. The spirit of sport is not defined anywhere in the code so this leaves the door open for WADA to place any substance in the banned list. When these criteria are considered, one realises there is no substance that is safe for anyone to take, including food. What will WADA do about recreational drugs? Will it be an arbiter of lifestyle as well? . . .

A System Biased Against Athletes

The drug test is performed by WADA and the suspicions raised are pursued by WADA. The judge is WADA or a WADA appointee. If there is to be a jury, that too will be a selection by WADA. This is highly unbalanced and needs revision. The application of WADA rules is not uniform over the world. In Australia the athlete who is chosen for a random drug test is to be pursued by the police to ensure their attendance for testing. This gives a sinister aspect to the whole picture. The statement the athlete has nothing to worry about if no drugs have been used does nothing to relieve anxiety. Police involvement is not a universal approach and unfairly penalises the affected athlete. As WADA has links to the IOC, there will always be some suspicion attached to this type of management.

It appears several basic legal rights afforded to most citizens of the world no longer apply to athletes when it comes to doping in sport. It is no longer necessary for an athlete to test positive as even "non-analytical positives" (perhaps hearsay?) are grounds for banning an athlete from competition.

To whom shall the penalty apply? WADA states the athlete is responsible for anything that is present in the body. This ignores the possibility of a planned attack on an individual by contaminating the food eaten. It is easy to distract an individual at meal time and then sprinkle a powder on the food to make the subject test positive. Similarly, sprinkling a drug over food at a buffet meal would be easy to do and render athletes drug positive indiscriminately. How could an athlete avoid this? . . .

The Best Solution to the Problem

There is nothing to suggest that doping will ever be eliminated. There has been no effort made to clean up the area that would inspire confidence. The best available option at this time is a harm reduction program. This would involve medical expertise of the highest calibre instead of those practitioners who are on the fringe of illegality. It would render the profit margins for illegal providers unattractive and gradually eliminate them from their markets, which will cease to exist. Athletes would receive better advice and would use less drug. There would be more investigation of drug effects and a better application of knowledge for the benefit of all. There is a challenge for all sporting bodies to establish a system that offers the same opportunity to all in a free and open spirit. Have they the courage to face up to it?

EVALUATING THE AUTHOR'S ARGUMENTS:

In questioning the value of drug testing in sports, Anthony P. Millar contends that illegal drug compounds can be found in everyday foods and that some legal drugs and foods can produce effects similar to those of banned substances. Do you agree with Millar that these accusations suggest that drug testing cannot be trusted to differentiate between users and nonusers? Explain how this view affects your own opinion of drug testing.

Severe Punishments for Drug-Positive Athletes Infringe on Individual Rights

"Is it ethical and morally right to sentence someone to a lengthy prison term for putting substances in their own body?"

Anthony Papa

In the following viewpoint, Anthony Papa, an activist against the government's war on drugs and manager of media relations for the Drug Policy Alliance, voices his objections to the trial (leading to eventual imprisonment in April 2011) of Barry Bonds, a San Francisco Giants outfielder and home run record holder who was charged in 2007 with lying about steroid use.

Pointing out that Bonds has continually denied knowingly taking steroids (he supposedly unwittingly took steroids from his trainer Greg Anderson), Papa sees the relentless persecution of Bonds as a useless attempt by the government to stop drug use in sports through severe punishments. Papa claims it is an infringement of personal liberties to dictate what substances people can put in their own bodies and that the war on drugs is really just a "war on people."

AS YOU READ, CONSIDER THE FOLLOWING QUESTIONS:
1. What does Papa believe is the real reason the government was trying Bonds in 2011?
2. Who is Randy Lanier and why is he important to Papa's argument?
3. Before steroids were banned in the 1970s, what percentage of Olympic athletes had used them, according to Papa?

[P]rofessional trainer] Greg Anderson, the government's key witness against baseball great Barry Bonds, refused to testify in court this week [in March 2011], landing him in jail for the fifth time. U.S. District Court Judge Susan Illston found Bonds' personal trainer in contempt of court. His lawyer says Anderson will not testify, leaving the government's case against Bonds very weak. In my view Anderson is a hero and a true stand up guy who is willing

Baseball Fans Respond to Barry Bonds's Drug Charge

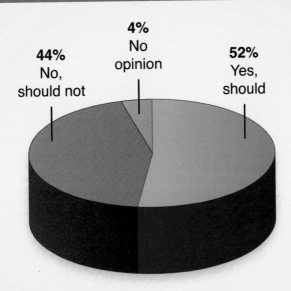

Should Major League Baseball officials take away Barry Bonds's batting records, including the record for most home runs in a single season, if they determine that Bonds used steroids?

44% No, should not

4% No opinion

52% Yes, should

Taken from: Gallup poll, March 10–12, 2006. www.gallup.com.

to sacrifice his own freedom to stop the imprisonment of Bonds for putting a substance in his body.

A Flurry of Scandal

Bonds returned to the same courthouse where he told a grand jury in December 2003 that he had never knowingly taken performance-enhancing substances. His lawyer confirmed this by suggesting in court that Bonds never lied to a grand jury and even admitted that he may have unwittingly used steroids.

Let's face it, Bonds' indictment for lying to a grand jury may be the legal basis of the government wanting to put the baseball legend in prison, but the real underlying reason for this federal indictment 8 years after the BALCO investigation is their failure to get Bonds to admit he had used steroids or any other performance-enhancing drugs. In that case, Bay Area Laboratory Co-Operative (BALCO) was

Former baseball star Barry Bonds's (center) conviction in the BALCO steroid investigations is seen by some as a useless attempt by authorities to stop drug use in sports through severe punishments.

alleged to have distributed illegal performance-enhancing drugs [to Bonds, among others], triggering investigations by several governmental agencies. This resulted in a huge scandal which involved many major league baseball players and led to Major League Baseball initiating penalties for players caught using steroids in 2004.

Bonds is facing prison time if convicted. Anti-doping advocates are hoping this will happen and use Bonds as an example to those calling for jail time for baseball players who use steroids. Many say that it may be the only effective deterrent for curbing illegal use.

Imprisonment Will Not Stop Drug Use

The government is willing to take down Bonds and in doing so blemish baseball so they can push their personal zero-tolerance agenda for drug use. They are set to call on Barry Bonds' former teammates to testify along with other retired Major League Baseball players in order to nail Bonds to a cross. What's next? Maybe exhuming the buried bones of all-star Ken Caminiti who died of a heart attack at age 41 after admitting taking steroids to boost his career.

Jailing Bonds will not solve baseball's problem or curb drug use in America. The United States has the highest incarceration rate in the world. It has 5 percent of the world's population, but 25 percent of the world's prisoners, with more than 2.4 million citizens sitting behind bars. Many of them have been rotting away in prison for years. One prisoner in particular I have come to know is former race car driver Randy Lanier, who is in prison serving a life sentence for marijuana. He is in his 23rd year of incarceration and is currently seeking clemency from President [Barack] Obama. Despite all of the incarceration, drug use and drug availability are as prevalent as ever.

Infringing Individual Rights

For the sake of argument, what if Bonds did use steroids? Does he belong in prison? He is not the first athlete to use them and he will not be the last. The pursuit for athletic superiority through the use of chemicals has been around a long time. Before steroids were officially banned in the early 1970s, almost 70 percent of all Olympic athletes had used them.

Is it ethical and morally right to sentence someone to a lengthy prison term for putting substances in their own body? The premise for prosecuting the other war with no exit strategy—the drug war—has slowly but surely infiltrated the public's eye through different vehicles. Now the feds attempt to bring their message through the sport of baseball.

Because of the government's stance against the use of drugs, Barry Bonds has joined the ranks of those demonized. This includes medical marijuana users, pain sufferers and their doctors who prescribe opioid analgesics, and students who are forced to urinate in cups. All of this in the name of a drug-free America without concern for individuals' rights. The war on drugs is a war on people. Let Barry Bonds be!

EVALUATING THE AUTHOR'S ARGUMENTS:

Anthony Papa claims that drug testing in sports has been influenced by the larger "war on drugs" in America. In his view, the purpose of both these "unwinnable" wars is for government to control what a person can and cannot put into his or her own body. Do you think Papa's connection between the drug wars in and out of sports is valid? What evidence can you cite from this book to support your claim?

Severe Punishments for Drug-Positive Athletes Could Have Unintended Consequences

"Taking a decision to ban an athlete for two years can be done a little more lightly than sending that same athlete to prison and preventing them from ever competing again!"

Ross Tucker

Ross Tucker is a research associate in the health sciences at the University of Cape Town in South Africa. He holds a doctorate in physical education and cowrites The Science of Sport, a website devoted to sports and athleticism. In the following viewpoint taken from that website, Tucker acknowledges that many athletes and sports authorities wish to maintain some integrity in sports by enacting bans on competitors who take performance-enhancing drugs. While Tucker admits his own belief that drug takers should be punished, he worries that because the methods of testing are not perfected and because legal challenges could mire the drug testing system and make it appear faulty, increasing punishments for drug offences may bring the whole system down. Tucker advocates for lighter punishments so that drug testing can continue to stand at least as a warning and a deterrent to those athletes who might be contemplating drug use.

AS YOU READ, CONSIDER THE FOLLOWING QUESTIONS:
1. What kinds of punishment does Tucker claim Lord Sebastian Coe and members of the IOC have suggested to contend with drug users?
2. Why does the author believe that harsher drug sentences will lead to court trials of athletes?
3. How does Tucker's "businessman" analogy help him think about the issue of punishments for drugs in sports?

Yesterday [February 25, 2008], we looked at the case of Dwain Chambers, disgraced sprinter from Britain who served a two year suspension for his use of the designer steroid THG [tetrahydrogestrinone] and who is now making a bid to run for Britain, first at the World Indoors (which he will run in) and then in the Olympic Games (where he's trying to get to). Even failing this, he's likely to push for the World Champs and other big races in the future. His desire to do so has sparked lively reactions, polarizing opinion among present and former athletes for Britain.

For example, double Olympic Champion Kelly Holmes has said:

This was an athlete who went to America, knowingly took a drug that was undetectable at the time, got caught, admitted he'd taken drugs, then went on to say that you can't win anything without taking drugs. It doesn't put us in a good light allowing a cheat, who has admitted he's a cheat, to represent us.

She is backed up by Steve Cram, former 1500m champion, and now a commentator and journalist, who suggests that a lifetime ban for any drug cheat should be in order:

I think a lot of us in the sport feel that a two-year ban is never enough for people committing that type of offence. And I would hope that as the next few months follow on, this isn't really just about Dwain Chambers at all, it's about the sport's attitude towards those who've committed serious drugs offences.

As things stand, Chambers will never take part in the Olympic Games, because the British Olympic Authorities do issue a lifetime ban to all convicted drug cheats. So for now, Cram, Holmes, and others who agree [with] them, can be satisfied knowing that the Olympics, at least, are out of reach.

However, there are those who support Chambers and are fully behind his efforts to run again. In effect, they are saying that "he has done the time, now let him come back and make a new start". They apply the letter of the law, which says that a convicted doper gets two years, and then is allowed to return to sport.

For example, Kim Collins, former 100m world champion, is quoted as saying:

> If they don't pick him then UK Athletics would be bending their own rules. He should be allowed to run and he should be representing Great Britain because he's the man for the job. He did serve his time and unless they are willing to change the rules and keep it 'once and you're out', he should be able to run.

Now, bear in mind that all this has been said against the backdrop of the issue of Chambers' selection of the British team for the world indoor championships in March, so people are commenting more on that issue than perhaps the issue of what to do with a convicted doper.

Those Supporting Harsh Punishments

But it got me thinking about the severity of the punishment for a doping offence. This issue, as you might imagine, is debated extensively, and some have suggested that any positive test should result in a lifetime ban, or at the very least, a four-year ban, as [Olympic gold medalist and vice president of the International Association of Athletics Federations] Lord Sebastian Coe and [former Olympian and sports administrator] Ed Moses have recently suggested.

Coe, for his part, has been pushing for a four-year ban for drug cheats since last year. If that sounds extreme, others within the IOC

[International Olympic Committee] have even suggested that doping offences should be criminalized—jail time the result of a positive test.

What interests me about this is that no one is looking at the testing procedure and systems, but rather assuming that testing is capable of reliably catching athletes who do cheat. For the implicit assumption when one calls for increased bans is that the process that will ultimately give that ban is sound, and not likely to collapse under what would become even more pressure to be correct. If the system for testing and then processing positive tests is even slightly flawed, increasing the bans simply invites even more legal wrangling and controversy.

Now, believe me, I'm the last person to side with those who cheat in sport—I wish we could watch sport knowing that the most any athlete is using is a Vitamin C supplement! But the problem is that the process AFTER A POSITIVE TEST seems to be so flawed that if the punishment was made more severe, the already creaky structures under which athletes are tested would come crashing down under the "burden of proof" that would be required to send a runner to jail!

A System Under Scrutiny

I recently read John Grisham's book "The Innocent Man", which is about a man who is wrongfully sentenced to death as a result of a flawed justice system—he loses 11 years of his life on death row before being exonerated. It would take me pages to run through just how flawed the system was, and besides, this is The Science of Sport, not a Book Club (though I'd highly recommend the book)! But the point is, it would be terrible if someone could write a book in 2015 about an athlete who spends 2 years in jail and/or is banned for life for testing positive for any drug, when he's actually been wrongfully convicted!

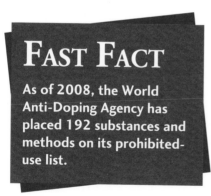

FAST FACT

As of 2008, the World Anti-Doping Agency has placed 192 substances and methods on its prohibited-use list.

Now, if you're thinking I'm going soft on dopers, let me address the balance. Because while the chance of "false positive" is a real one, what concerns me more is that dopers who test positive will have even more chance of getting away with it, because the entire process that

"I am not now, nor have I in the past ever knowingly taken any steroids."

ultimately delivers their sentence would now be under even more pressure to avoid a false conviction.

What we have seen in recent years is a dramatic change in how doping cases are managed. In the past, it was a case that an athlete would test positive, receive their ban, and disappear for four years—think [Canadian sprinter] Ben Johnson in 1988. He got caught, took his punishment [i.e., was stripped of his Olympic medals and banned from competition for two years], and we didn't hear from him again, until the ban was served.

But what is happening more and more today is that athletes are wising up to the "grey areas" in the system. There is almost a "guide book" on how to respond when you test positive. You begin by attacking the personality and integrity of your accusers, you go after the credibility of the laboratory testing you, you cry out that people are out to get

Lord Sebastian Coe, vice president of the International Association of Athletics Federations and former Olympic runner, believes that any athlete testing positive for doping should get a lifetime or, at the very least, a four-year suspension from competing.

you and that you're being discriminated against. Then you take your defence into the media and put all kinds of articles on Wikipedia to claim your innocence. You might even consider writing a book about it, and you definitely hire an expensive legal team who help you concoct defences like the "vanishing twin theory" which is more at home on an episode of "House" than in a sports tribunal, or you simply bombard the system with so much doubt that you escape punishment because no one can prove the use amidst all that uncertainty. And all the while, you deny, deny, deny, because actually proving that you used drugs is no longer as simple as testing your blood or urine and finding the presence of drugs in it! (and this doesn't even take into account the fact that a lot of drugs can't even be detected!)

Maintaining the Upper Hand

The positive drugs test, formerly definitive proof that an athlete has doped, is now nothing more than the start of a usually messy, drawn out fight that is played out in the media and undermines the sport more than even the drugs use does. The problem is that sometimes the athlete has a case, because there are flaws and mistakes, and the system is not beyond reproach, which it needs to be in order to issue life bans. The result of this is that I honestly believe that we are headed for the day where an athlete who tests positive will face a trial consisting of a judge and a jury of their peers, who will have to assess their guilt based on days of testimony and evidence . . . think [TV series] "Boston Legal" and "The Practice" for sport.

So my concern with increasing the length of a doping ban, and possibly criminalizing the use of drugs in sport is that the testing procedures, which are already "losing their teeth" in terms of actually following through with a positive test, will become completely toothless as a result of increased bans—taking a decision to ban an athlete for two years can be done a little more lightly than sending that same athlete to prison and preventing them from ever competing again!

So while in theory and principle I'm all for a lifetime ban or even criminal charges, actually proving it poses a problem, and until WADA [World Anti-Doping Agency] and the federations figure out how to regain the upper hand in the "post-positive test" battle, increasing the ban will do little more than intensify the pressure they are under.

But let's get back to Dwain Chambers, for as Cram points out, the issue is not solely about one athlete, but about the attitude of the system towards its "cheats". And I'd love to hear from any of our readers who have some sports experience, or even some experience in employment law on this one, because the issue here is bordering on that of "restraint of trade", where someone is prevented from earning a living unfairly. . . .

I tried to think of the analogy from the world of business—if a businessman was caught defrauding his company, he'd without doubt be fired, and probably face criminal charges. But would he ever be able to work in the same industry again? Would the business world consider issuing a lifetime ban on a corrupt businessman? Well, rhetorical question, because there's no "system" to ban him from. But there's a good chance he'd be labeled and unable to find work, at least in the same area. Is that the same situations as Chambers and the Olympic Games?

All questions for which I don't have an answer.

EVALUATING THE AUTHOR'S ARGUMENTS:

Ross Tucker maintains that harsh punishments for drug violations in sports might undermine the reason for drug bans in the first place. Explain why Tucker believes this. Then explain whether you think his argument is strong enough to convince authorities to impose lighter penalties for drug use.

Athletes Should Be Punished for Recreational Drug Use

Henry Winter

> "Cocaine warrants a suspension whenever it enters a footballer's body. It is illegal."

In the following viewpoint, Henry Winter, the European football, or soccer, correspondent for the British newspaper the *Daily Telegraph*, claims that sports authorities and the government should punish athletes for recreational drug use. In Winter's opinion, sports figures are role models who are held to antidrug policies while on the field of competition and should retain those standards of integrity while off the field. According to current rules in the United Kingdom, athletes are only tested for stimulants like cocaine when they are "in competition"— within a few hours of a match. By not testing "out of competition" athletes for recreational drugs, Winter maintains, sports authorities are seemingly condoning such use and sending the wrong message to other athletes and to society at large.

AS YOU READ, CONSIDER THE FOLLOWING QUESTIONS:
1. What sports does Winter argue are more susceptible to drug use than European football?
2. Why does Winter claim that United Kingdom sports authorities have an ethical stake in fighting the larger drug problem in society?
3. As Andy Parkinson explains in Winter's viewpoint, why does cocaine fail to meet the World Anti-Doping Agency's criteria for substances that can be banned "out of competition"?

Cocaine ruins relationships, divides families and triggers heart attacks yet under anti-doping laws a professional footballer can pump his veins full of the stuff the day before a game, snort enough to blow his nasal septum away, and still not fail a drugs test because he is "out of competition".

If he takes cocaine 24 hours later, when deemed "in competition", a two-year ban awaits. This inconsistency screams out to be corrected.

Applying new tests laid down by the World Anti-Doping Agency [WADA], the fabulous beaker boys from UK Sport will be visiting more footballers [soccer players] more frequently from July 1 [2008].

Testing Is a Reminder

UK Sport's crusade should, of course, be welcomed even if football is not afflicted by the drug epidemic that blights other high-stakes pursuits like track and field and the Tour de France.

FAST FACT

Drug-monitoring services can detect cocaine in a player's urine up to five days after use.

Footballers need to be reminded of the perils of drug consumption, whether performance-enhancing or recreational. Diego Maradona [an Argentinian footballer suspended in 1991] and Adrian Mutu [a Romanian footballer who failed a drug test in 2004] played Russian roulette with their health when dabbling with cocaine, and also tarnished their profession's image.

So if cocaine is a menace on match-day, which UK Sport rightly rule it is, it must also be a menace the rest of the time. When fans talk of Maradona's infamous cocaine habit, they do not differentiate whether he took cocaine while heading for the game or when off-duty. He took drugs. Period.

Sending the Right Message

UK Sport's responsibility is to clean up sport, not society, but as a publicly-funded body, and an organization full of sensible people aware that sportsmen and women are role models, they should surely see the broader picture.

Society has a drug problem and it transmits the wrong message for sport to argue that cocaine is only wrong depending on the day. Cocaine warrants a suspension whenever it enters a footballer's body. It is illegal.

Government should use sport in the fight to warn people of the hazards of polluting blood-streams with chemicals. They should enlist the support of leading footballers to promote the virtues of being clean.

Andy Parkinson, head of UK Sport's antidoping office says his organization runs two tests for cocaine use: one for "in competition" and one for "out of competition." Violations of the former are prosecuted but not of the latter, which the author believes is wrong.

The Health Risks Associated with Cocaine Use

Adverse Physical Health Effects of Cocaine

- Strokes
- Convulsions/seizures
- Chronic headaches
- Tremors/twitching
- Spontaneous abortions
- Chronic irritation of nasal membranes
- Abnormal vision/blindness
- Sexual dysfunction
- Elevated blood pressure/elevated pulse rate
- Hepatitis and AIDS from use of needles
- Death

Taken from: ESPN.com, "Cocaine." September 6, 2007. http://espn.go.com.

UK Sport and the FA [Football Association] are currently drawing up a list of 30 England and other high-profile footballers to undergo regular testing; these should be seen as ambassadors for a drug-free sport (assuming none fail tests).

If footballers are to be role models, they must be drug-free throughout the year, not simply when "on duty". But UK Sport view cocaine as a "stimulant" and consider only its impact on the player's sporting performance.

"Cocaine is only banned 'in competition'," explains Andy Parkinson, UK Sport's Head of Operations for a Drug-Free Sport. "Out of competition, cocaine is not banned. It is a stimulant that only stays in your system for eight hours."

UK Sport run tests on two separate "menus" of drugs, "in competition" and "out of competition". Parkinson adds: "For 'in-competition', it is everything on the [WADA] list.

"The FA define 'in competition' as from midnight on the day of the game and it concludes half an hour after the final whistle. We'd pick that up and prosecute the athlete. 'Out of competition', there is no performance value in taking a stimulant."

Tarnishing the Spirit of Sport

So when UK Sport's testers arrive at a player's home on a non-match-day or a Caribbean resort in the summer to check whether anything proscribed lurks in a player's urine or blood, they will not look for cocaine.

"We would only run an 'out-of-competition' screen on the sample, which wouldn't even try and test for cocaine, because it is a stimulant," Parkinson continues.

Parkinson then makes an important point in saying: "Cocaine is on the banned list because it meets two of the three criteria to be included on the list: performance enhancing, damages the athlete's health or contravenes the spirit of sport."

As a stimulant, cocaine may not be performance-enhancing "out of competition" but it clearly has long-term health issues as well as trampling all over the "spirit of sport".

The nightmare scenario for the FA is an England player being caught taking cocaine on his day off by the police or the tabloids and facing only a slap-on-the-wrist disrepute charge from the footballing authorities.

This glaring loophole in the drug rules needs closing. For football's sake—and society's.

> **EVALUATING THE AUTHOR'S ARGUMENTS:**
>
> What is the basis of Henry Winter's argument that recreational drug use should not be tolerated among athletes? Read Allen Fox's viewpoint in this chapter and explain how the two authors see the issue differently.

Athletes Should Not Be Punished for Recreational Drug Use

*"If athletes
... are
willing
to accept
the health
risks [of
recreational
drug use or
other habits],
foolish as this
may be, what
business
is it of the
authorities to
punish them
for doing so?"*

Allen Fox

Lecturer and sports consultant Allen Fox is a former professional tennis player. In the viewpoint that follows, Fox claims that banning athletes from competition— or otherwise punishing them—for recreational drug use is unfair. He insists that sports authorities should have no power over what an athlete puts into his or her own body as long as the substance is not a performance enhancer. According to Fox, drugs like marijuana and cocaine have no significant positive effect on play and therefore their use should not result in banning or suspension. Fox maintains that recreational drug use is a personal choice that, if left unchecked, might require rehabilitation and education but should not result in dismissal from athletic competition.

1. Why does Fox think it is unfair that cocaine, a stimulant, is marked as a prohibited substance in athletic drug testing?
2. How does the author suggest authorities solve the role model argument that is waged in response to leniency for recreational drug use?
3. According to Fox, why did it seem questionable for the Association of Tennis Professionals to refrain from punishing Andre Agassi for testing positive for drugs in 1997?

L et me be clear to start with that I am not advocating that athletes or anyone else indulge in cannabis, cocaine, or any other recreational drug. The health hazards of most are well-known and severe. I just think that banning athletes from participating in their sports or fining them for using recreational drugs is unreasonable and unfair. (This is just my opinion, of course, and I don't expect what I say here to cause any rule changes, but it will, hopefully, provide food for thought.)

An example of severe punishment was banning [tennis player] Martina Hingis, a five-time [Grand] Slam [tournament] winner, for two years for testing positive for cocaine at Wimbledon in 2007 and basically ending her career. They gave her the tennis death penalty. I have never been a Hingis fan because she was so cocky when she was winning Slams, making statements to the effect that players like Steffi Graf were old and over the hill and that she and the other young, pretty new players were taking over. (One of my fondest memories is of the 1999 French Open final when "old" and "over the hill" Steffi Graf, having suffered multiple knee operations, gave her a good whipping.) Nevertheless, I still feel Hingis' punishment was excessive.

Not Performance Enhancers

Performance-enhancing drugs: Ok, players using known performance-enhancing drugs like the anabolic agents—Andro, Norandrosterone, Nandrolone, etc.—should obviously be banned. There is no reasonable argument in their favor. These drugs build muscle mass and strength [and] give the users an unfair competitive advantage. But recreational drugs are a totally different matter.

Recreational drugs: Since "recreational" drugs are labeled as such rather than as "performance enhancing" I'm not sure what the rationale is for punishing athletes for using them. There is no convincing evidence that they help performance (otherwise they'd be labeled as "performance enhancing"). In fact, from what information I could gather, I would guess they are more likely to hurt performance rather than help it. Of course, nobody knows the true effects on athletic performance of drugs like cannabis, cocaine, and methamphetamine (or nicotine and caffeine, for that matter) so my guess is as good as anybody's. And it's hard for me to imagine how cannabis, which is classified as a psychoactive drug (meaning it changes perception and other brain functions), could be helpful to one's tennis game. If my livelihood were on the line I would be scared to death playing while high on cannabis.

Cocaine is a stimulant, as is methamphetamine, but so are nicotine and caffeine. Most tournament players are jittery enough to begin with and need to relax more than to be revved up. Andre Agassi stated in his book, "Open," that he took crystal meth when he was at a mental low point. He thought it would hurt his game, but did it anyway, partially because it would hurt his game, and at the time he hated tennis. In any case, the actions of these stimulants are relatively immediate and short term, so getting high the night before wouldn't increase a player's energy during the match—in fact, quite the opposite since there is often a rebound effect of exhaustion.

Judgment Calls

Stimulants during matches: Maybe taking stimulants during a match— for example, in the fifth set when you are tiring—should be a punishable event. (Of course there is no evidence that the banned players were doing this.) Arguing against this is the fact that players are already allowed to take various legal stimulants during matches—caffeinated beverages like Coke, coffee, or tea—but they usually don't because the experts think they are better off with sports drinks containing nutrients and electrolytes. In fact Michael Bergeron, Ph.D. advised against, during play, using energy drinks like Red Bull in the March 2010 *Tennis* magazine, saying, "there's a lot of negative things that can also go with these drinks." Too much caffeine, for example, can make you jittery and hurt your game. "I'd rather see tennis players get their energy from eating right and resting well," he says.

Rationale for taking action against athletes using recreational drugs: Joseph de Pencier, of the Canadian Centre for Ethics in Sport, states the reason for banning recreational drugs like cannabis: "If you accept the premise that doping can involve health risks, doping can involve actions contrary to the spirit of sport, quite apart from the performance enhancement, then treating cannabinoids in this way is quite

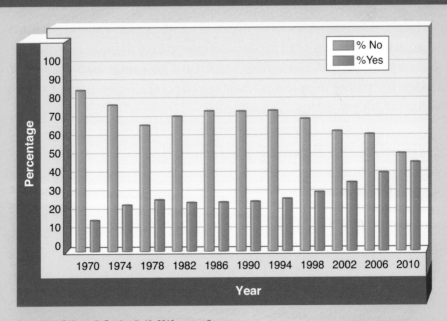

Support for Legalization of Marijuana Is Growing

Do you think the use of marijuana should be made legal?

Taken from: Gallup poll, October 7–10, 2010. www.gallup.com.

Martina Hingis speaks to the press after her two-year ban from competition by the International Tennis Association for cocaine use. The ban effectively ended her career.

justified." My translation of his statement is that they are banned because they are bad for you and because using them is not nice. He could have added the usual arguments for banning: athletes are role models for young people and their use of recreational drugs, many of which are illegal, sets a bad example.

Examining the Banning Rationale

Rationale for not taking action against athletes: I would like to discuss here each reason usually given for punishing athletes, one reason at a time, and show that they make little sense.

1. *Because they are bad for the athlete's health.* This is almost too absurd to justify a counter argument. Protecting the athlete's health is up to the athlete himself or herself (and maybe their trainers, parents,

coaches, etc.). It is reasonable for the authorities to voice concerns, kind people that they are, but not to punish transgressions. McDonalds hamburgers, Twinkies, cigarettes, scuba-diving, motorcycle-riding, spare-ribs, candy bars and about 1000 other things are bad for an athlete's health or pose health risks. If athletes want to eat these things or do these things and are willing to accept the health risks, foolish as this may be, what business is it of the authorities to punish them for doing so?

2. *Because they are illegal.* Speeding in one's car is also illegal as is not paying one's taxes. How about a D.W.I. [citation for driving while intoxicated]? Misguided as these choices may be, many people do it anyway and are willing to risk the consequences which, if they are caught, will be imposed by the legal authorities after trial in a court of law. The tennis authorities are simply piling on in an area that is not their business.

3. *Because athletes are role models for young people and are setting a bad example:* The authorities could solve the role model problem by simply not testing for recreational drugs in the first place. Then nobody would know, and there would be no bad example. It is also unhelpful, if this is the issue (which, of course, it isn't), to share positive test results with the media and public.

Moreover, people in other highly publicized vocations—politicians, movie stars, rock stars, etc.—are also role models. Why are they not also drug-tested and banned from their professions if they are found to be users? Why single out athletes? In addition, the most frequently used recreational drug is alcohol, but even though it's legal, drinking it still sets a bad example since it can lead to alcoholism. Smoking sets an even worse example, as nicotine is highly addictive and a killer over time. Should athletes be banned from their sport for setting the bad example of drinking alcohol, smoking, or eating McDonalds hamburgers?

4. *Because it runs counter to the spirit of the sport.* This argument is the vaguest of all. I'm not sure who gets to define what the "spirit of the sport" is or should be. (I suppose the authorities are.) I'm also not sure what the proper penalty should be for acting counter to the questionably determined "spirit of the sport," but giving Hingis the athletic death penalty strikes me as excessive.

Since the usual reasons given for punishing athletes for using recreational drugs (as stated above) seem spurious (at least to my logic system), I would like to put forth the only plausible explanation I can think of. I suspect they may have simply mixed together in their minds performance enhancing and recreational drugs. They repeated the mantra "Drugs are bad, drugs are bad!" so many times that they unconsciously felt impelled to apply the same punishments for both without further thought. Having already decided to punish recreational drug use, they then scrambled afterward to come up with plausible reasons to justify themselves. It is a version of "ready, shoot, aim."

Arbitrary Application

Finally, the authorities seem to be rather flexible in their acceptance of excuses for failing their drug tests and in their application of penalties. (When they are protecting something as vague as the "spirit of the sport' they buy themselves a great deal of leeway.) For example, in 1997 when Andre Agassi tested positive for drugs he lied and claimed he had accidently and unknowingly drunk from an associate's spiked drink (a likely story), and asked for understanding and leniency. After due consideration, the ATP [Association of Tennis Professionals] decided against imposing any penalties at all. (After all, boys will be boys!) I know this may sound cynical, but could their decision have been influenced by the fact that Agassi was the biggest name in the game and a huge draw at the gate and with the sponsors? Hingis, on the other hand, was well past her prime and on the way down when her harsh penalty was imposed.

Coincidentally, they also gave the athletic death penalty (a two year suspension) to unknown New Zealander, Mark Nielsen, in 2006 for using finasteride, a drug that reduces hair loss. (In fact, I use it myself, and it hasn't helped my game a bit.) They claimed that failure to check if the medication might contain a prohibited substance "indicates a serious dereliction of duty on the part of any player who participates in a sport governed by the WADA [World Anti-Doping Agency] Code." Their attitude was, "We've got to make an example of him." So "Off with his head!" You will have noted, I'm sure, that Nielsen was not a household name nor was he a strong factor in enhancing gate receipts. It strikes me that unequal doses of self-interest on the part of tennis authorities make for unequal dispensations of justice.

Unfortunately, we all do lots of things that aren't good for us. We have choices and we often make wrong ones. It's too bad, but hopefully we learn to do better in the future. If we don't, then it's too bad for us. But in my opinion we should have the freedom to do these things as long as we don't hurt others. The authorities should protect me from your acts that can hurt me, but not from my acts that can hurt me. In summary, my feelings on the use of recreational drugs, be it by athletes or anyone else, is that it's mostly a problem for the user himself or herself. To the extent it doesn't hurt anybody else or give an unfair advantage in sport, it would seem that it calls for rehabilitation and education rather than punishment.

EVALUATING THE AUTHOR'S ARGUMENTS:

Why does Allen Fox contend that the illegality of recreational drugs in society is not grounds for sports authorities to punish athletes caught using these drugs? Do you think recreational drug use is part of an athlete's private life or should it be publicly identified as an intolerable blemish on one's sporting career? Explain your answer using the claims expressed in this viewpoint.

Chapter 3

Is Drug Testing for Student Athletes Necessary and Effective?

A laboratory technician holds a sample tube of an athlete's urine to test for banned substances.

The Case for Mandatory Drug Testing for College Athletes

"University athletes in the NCAA a lot of the time turn to performance enhancing drugs, and that is why it should be mandatory for drug testing."

Zack Hurd

Zack Hurd is a competitive swimmer and former NCAA (National Collegiate Athletic Association) athlete. In the following viewpoint, Hurd claims that the pressures of academic life and the need to perform well in competition weigh on student athletes and contribute to performance-enhancing-drug use in college sports. However, Hurd also blames the NCAA for not taking action for its own mistakes and not doing enough to discourage drug use and educate athletes about its dangers. For these reasons, he maintains that college authorities should routinely test their athletes for drugs.

AS YOU READ, CONSIDER THE FOLLOWING QUESTIONS:
 1. Why does Hurd claim that the drug-education class athletes are
    required to take in some colleges does not achieve its aim?
 2. According to Hurd, what is the main "competition" that stu-
    dent athletes face while living the collegiate life?
 3. Why does the author think that drug use among collegiate ath-
    letes will only get worse over time?

Citius, Altius, Fortius: Faster, Higher, Stronger, the Olympic
motto, the dream of every young athlete around the world,
to reach the ultimate stage in sport and hear those words
said under the Olympic flag while surrounded by athletes from
across the world. As a young athlete you would also hope that when
you finally reached that ultimate level, that you yourself made it
fairly and that all the athletes that share that stage got to the games
in the same way.

As we all know this is not the case; even iconic athletes that all of
us would like to see have their name carried on forever are brought
down due to past or current drug use.

Marian Jones is a great example of an athlete who we all would have
hoped and thought was just a supreme human being. But what brings
athletes to this level, to the level of using performance enhancing
drugs to further their success? What changes the mindset from that
childhood dream of being the best that you can be in one's own skin,
to jeopardizing everything to have the upper hand over unknowing
opponents?

Sure drug use can be a problem at any level of sport, but not until
the University level is it more widely used. The availability is there,
the pressures are there, and the stress and outside factors make drug
use the problem that it is.

When an athlete enters the realm of University sport they are very
unlikely to be prepared for the world they are entering. In the NCAA
the pressure from your team, from your coaches and from fans is
enough to bewilder anyone. There is a class that all student-athletes
take that is supposed to help them through their university experience,
to deal with gambling and drug use and how to deal with life in the

limelight. I can tell you from personal experience that this class is just a way to help the student-athletes get an easy A and further ensure that they can stay with the school. It is another way that the NCAA tries to get around the educational restraints, and by very little way is for the physical benefit of the athletes.

The pressure to perform is always on the back of the university athlete's mind, and this is where the problems with performance enhancing drugs come into play. The average university student finds it hard to make it day to day dealing with classes, money, living and food.

Now add in twenty plus hours of training a week and a scholarship that relies on your performance. For many student-athletes there is no money saved up, there is no work experience, that athlete's whole life has been devoted to sport and that's all that they might have. The majority of the athlete's competition may not be on the field, or in the pool or on the ice or may not even be in the classroom. The main competition is mental and knowing that at any time you could lose your spot to someone new or a cheaper find, if that happens what are you left with?

Where do you turn if you are in jeopardy of losing not only your dream now but the funding for your books, or food, or your living, or your education? This is when University athletes in the NCAA a lot of the time turn to performance enhancing drugs, and that is why it should be mandatory for drug testing.

> ## FAST FACT
>
> Even though about 1 percent of college athletes surveyed by the NCAA in 2006 admitted using steroids, that percentage is roughly triple the rate of steroid use among collegiate nonathletes.

There obviously are much deeper issues that need to be dealt with; the actual root of the problem needs to be addressed, because I do not agree that it is entirely the athlete's fault, a lot of the time they do not have any other options but until the NCAA is forced to take action for their own mistakes I believe that there will continue to be drug use and if anything this activity will only increase with higher demands and larger salaries at the end of the road.

Marion Jones answers questions outside a federal courthouse about her conviction for lying to federal agents about her drug use in 2007. She had to forfeit her Olympic gold medals from 2000.

I have lived the student-athlete life in the NCAA division I, and I know the amount of drug use that I know of personally. I did not even go to a large school with a big name: I can only speculate how much worse the problem and stresses can get.

EVALUATING THE AUTHOR'S ARGUMENTS:

Zack Hurd defends the routine drug testing of college athletes because he insists, as a former collegiate athlete, that student athletes often give in to social and personal pressures to use drugs. What are the pressures Hurd identifies? Do you think these pressures explain why most student athletes would turn to performance-enhancing drugs? Explain why or why not.

The Case Against Mandatory Drug Testing for College Athletes

Todd Pheifer

"While one doesn't necessarily want to say that drug testing in college is a bad idea, there are certainly some challenges to overcome."

In the viewpoint that follows, Todd Pheifer, a part-time writer and college teacher, claims that mandatory drug testing of college athletes is plagued with challenges. Pheifer states that drug testing is too expensive for many schools and that sports authorities have no clear guidelines on what drugs should and should not be banned from competition. Finally, Pheifer insists that drug testing is not a strong deterrent in an atmosphere that emphasizes winning at all costs.

AS YOU READ, CONSIDER THE FOLLOWING QUESTIONS:

1. According to Pheifer, what are collegiate sports supposed to be, but what, however, is the reality?
2. Why does the author insist that providing a list of banned substances is not a deterrent to scientists and athletes looking for an edge in sports?
3. Why might drug testing regulations be an unfair hindrance to smaller colleges, in Pheifer's opinion?

In an ideal world, all athletes would compete on a "level" playing field, particularly in the amateur ranks where sports is "supposed" to be an expression of the collegiate spirit. However, the reality of college sports is that it has become big business, both for the players and for the schools involved. Players feel tremendous pressure in particular sports to succeed and gain fame, which in certain sports can lead to large professional contracts. People increasingly have a sense that drug use is not isolated to a few select athletes, which has caused it to receive a sort of passive acceptance over time. Still, there are a lot of reasons why drug testing is difficult. While one doesn't necessarily want to say that drug testing in college is a bad idea, there are certainly some challenges to overcome.

Technology

One major difficulty with drug testing is the technology that is connected to the problem. If a governing body were to come up with a list of banned substances, scientists and athletes would probably find

Sealed containers holding athletes' drug test samples are prepared for shipment to a laboratory. Testing athletes is expensive, and not every school has the resources for widespread testing.

a way to start using something else. Many of the drugs of today can be designed in a such a way that they are not easily detected. In addition, there is the issue of agreement between various governing bodies, and consistency would be a major issue. Technically, an over-the-counter painkiller offers a chemical advantage so there are often blurred lines when it comes to what should be banned.

Drug Use by NCAA Division

Division I

Drug	Year			
	1993	1997	2001	2005
Amphetamines	2.1%	2.5%	3.2%	4.0%
Anabolic steroids	1.9%	1.2%	1.6%	1.2%
Ephedrine	N/A	3.0%	2.4%	2.4%
Nutritional supplements	N/A	N/A	46.0%	33.4%

Division II

Drug	Year			
	1993	1997	2001	2005
Amphetamines	2.0%	3.3%	3.3%	3.8%
Anabolic steroids	4.3%	1.1%	2.5%	1.2%
Ephedrine	N/A	4.2%	4.1%	2.6%
Nutritional supplements	N/A	N/A	41.5%	27.9%

Division III

Drug	Year			
	1993	1997	2001	2005
Amphetamines	1.9%	3.7%	3.7%	4.6%
Anabolic steroids	1.9%	1.3%	1.4%	1.0%
Ephedrine	N/A	3.8%	2.5%	2.6%
Nutritional supplements	N/A	N/A	39.8%	28.1%

Taken from: National Collegiate Athletic Association Staff. "NCAA Study of Substance Use Habits of College Student-Athletes." January 2006. www.ncaa.org.

Cost

Another major issue is the financial toll that drug testing would take on college sports. Testing bodily fluids for particular substances is not always cheap, and not every school has the financial resources for widespread testing. Professional sports leagues may be able to afford certain amounts of testing, but colleges do not always have the same budgets. Some smaller schools might be severely hampered if they had to bear the brunt of the cost.

FAST FACT

Although NCAA drug policy calls for mandatory drug testing of student athletes, universities are not required to have their own in-house policies, to implement supplementary drug education, nor to compel students to sign waivers granting permission to be tested.

Therefore, drug testing might be a good plan, but many ideas have good intent and still lack the funding to be truly implemented.

Root of the Problem

Again, the idea of drug testing and having some assurance of fairness is a good concept. However, the logistics, cost, and implementation is a definitively difficult task. Mandatory drug testing is one way of dealing with college athletics, but anytime there is competition, humans will look for an advantage. Unless people figure out a way to lessen the desire to win, there will always be a temptation to seek an unfair advantage, which makes drug testing just a symptom of a much larger problem found in the nature of humankind.

EVALUATING THE AUTHOR'S ARGUMENTS:

Todd Pheifer states that the human desire to win is the obstacle to successfully stopping college athletes from using performance-enhancing drugs. Do you believe that this argument is strong enough to call for a ban on mandatory drug tests at the college level? Why or why not? If not, what might be a better argument, in your opinion? Why?

AP Survey: College Drug-Testing All over the Map

Eddie Pells

"Not a single school's drug policy submitted to the AP read exactly the same as another— even within conferences and states—and the majority appeared much more concerned with curbing recreational drug use than steroids."

In the following viewpoint, Associated Press (AP) sports writer Eddie Pells reports his findings on what he claims are inconsistent and poorly enforced drug policies in college sports programs. Pells claims that the drug policies present in collegiate sports have no consistent ties. Some policies depend on the sport or the level of competition. Some tests cover not only recreational drugs, but also performance-enhancing drugs, while other college drug tests cover only the recreational drugs.

AS YOU READ, CONSIDER THE FOLLOWING QUESTIONS:

1. According to the article, is the University of Miami's drug testing program one of the more stringent and what is its drug testing policy and penalty?
2. Of the colleges that responded to the AP survey, what percentage say they have their own drug testing programs; what subgroup had 98 percent of schools with their own drug testing program, and what did they test for?
3. Which college is specifically mentioned in the article to be one of the few colleges that test for performance-enhancing drugs; what other kinds of substances does this college test for?

When it comes to college sports and drug testing, policies are as varied as the schools themselves.

An Associated Press survey of measures used by the NCAA, conferences and more than 50 schools to keep steroids and performance-enhancing drugs out of sports found policies all over the map—with no consistency or integrated strategy to tie them together.

While the NCAA runs an umbrella drug-testing program, the conferences vary widely in what they do to augment those rules. Some, like the Big Ten, have extensive guidelines that closely mirror the NCAA's. Others have nothing and say they simply adhere to the NCAA, which tests athletes on campus and at postseason events it sanctions, including the Final Four this week.

The AP sent out requests for information about drug-testing policies at 76 universities—73 in the six biggest conferences and three mid-major teams ranked in the Top 25 in the Feb. 28 AP men's basketball poll. It received responses from 51.

Some policies—like the one at Florida—were stringent, booting athletes who test positive for steroids into Phase IV of its sanction program, which calls for missing at least 50 percent of the season. Others barely mentioned performance-enhancing drugs. Not a single school's drug policy submitted to the AP read exactly the same as another—even within conferences and states—and the majority appeared much more concerned with curbing recreational drug use than steroids.

"They have programs," said Gary Wadler of the World Anti-Doping Agency. "Some are related to conferences, some related to championships, some depend on sports, some depend on drugs. But has anyone really taken a serious look at the NCAA the way we've looked at the NFL and Major League Baseball? The answer is no. For a long time, I've been mystified by that."

Michigan State athletic director Mark Hollis said developing good drug-testing programs "is an evolving process."

"As institutions, it seems we're always playing catch-up," Hollis said. "The effectiveness and costs of testing provide great challenges."

The NCAA program calls for at least one drug-testing visit to every Division I and Division II campus each school year—in which a number of athletes from various sports can be tested. The NCAA, which says it sanctions about 400,000 athletes across all divisions, administered about 11,000 tests in 2008–09, the most recent period for which statistics are available.

Beginning in August, a new NCAA rule will require all Division I schools to designate a staff member who can answer questions about dietary supplements and banned drugs.

The reputable National Center for Drug-Free Sport runs the NCAA testing program but does it according to guidelines approved by the NCAA, not the code established by WADA. The NCAA's rules about advance notice, independence in judging cases and transparency skew far from the WADA rules, which are what some of the most-respected experts view as best practices. When asked, the U.S. Anti-Doping Agency refused to run the NCAA's testing program.

The issue of doping in college sports was most vividly brought to light last year when Canada's Waterloo University shut down its football program for a season after nine players tested positive for performance-enhancing drugs.

Bob Copeland, the athletic director who ordered the entire team tested after one player was arrested for possession and trafficking anabolic steroids, was roundly criticized for his vigilance when the case broke. But the positive tests vindicated him.

In an interview with the AP, Copeland cited studies that say between 4 and 6 percent of high school students knowingly use anabolic steroids. He believes that if it was happening at his Canadian university, it's logical to think it's happening in the United States, where college sports are much bigger in almost every respect.

"If you had a mathematician looking at it from a purely logical point of view, you'd draw the conclusion that you'd think it's happening somewhere," Copeland said. "But you don't really know until you have a testing system that's rigorous, unannounced, with a lot of testing happening at different periods throughout the year."

U.S. college sports, though, have produced very little news about steroid problems. In the past year, only one case involving performance-enhancing drugs has made significant headlines—and they came and went quickly.

At almost the same time the Waterloo case produced the first North American athlete to test positive for human growth hormone, a University of Miami baseball player was charged with possession of marijuana and 19 vials of human growth hormone. He was dismissed from the team, and every member of the team was tested, with no one showing any indication of either recreational or performance-enhancing drug usage.

The AP review found Miami's drug-testing program to be one of the more stringent, calling for a minimum of three urine tests a year and automatic suspensions after the first positive test.

But there was nothing in the policy that called for blood testing. It was not included in any of the college policies reviewed by the AP. Part of that is because of expense—which can range up to $800 per test including collection, testing and analysis—and part of it is because "there are a lot of challenges to collecting blood," said Mary Wilfert, the NCAA's associate director of health and safety.

"We don't think we're at a point yet where we believe it's considered critical to do it, and membership hasn't demanded it yet," Wilfert said.

Neither the NFL nor Major League Baseball has blood testing, either—considered by experts to be a major flaw in their programs.

Among the NCAA program's other perceived weaknesses are lack of no-advance-notice testing and a penalty structure that calls for a one-year suspension for a first offense, as opposed to two under the WADA code.

Wilfert says the association's sanctioning policy is based on the fact that college players only have four years of eligibility, while at the Olympic level "participation is for as long as the body can manage it."

On the lack of no-advance-notice testing—something WADA experts consider crucial but is nonetheless rarely seen outside the Olympic movement—Wilfert conceded the NCAA has not reached that point, "but if you believe you could be tested at any time, you're less likely to use."

Wilfert said the NCAA, as in all things it oversees, molds policies according to what members desire.

Judging by a recent NCAA survey about drug-testing in sports, there's only lukewarm interest. In 2009, the NCAA sent out about 1,000 49-question surveys and received responses from only 45 percent of the schools.

Of those who responded, 54 percent said they had their own drug-testing program in place. That number jumped to 98 percent—55 of 56 respondents—for schools in Division I BCS [Bowl Championship Series] football. But of those, only 18 percent tested for anabolic steroids, while 99 percent tested for marijuana and cocaine.

Michigan, with one of the nation's biggest athletic departments, is one of the few schools that tests for performance-enhancing drugs.

"It's a very complete test that covers not only recreational drugs, but also steroids and the misuse of prescription drugs and other drugs deemed illegal or as performance-enhancers by the NCAA," said Wolverines athletic director Dave Brandon "Our student-athletes and coaches know we don't just talk the talk. We walk the walk."

EVALUATING THE AUTHOR'S ARGUMENTS:

This article quotes an athletic director who claims that if doping was happening at a high school level within Canada, it is logical to believe it is happening within the United States as well. Does the author endorse this claim? Why or why not? How does this relate to the NCAA rules? The author points out differences between WADA and NCAA rules for testing. Make a list of the differences and determine whether the author has a preference for one set or the other. Explain your analysis with information from the viewpoint.

Viewpoint

4

Educators Should Be Held to the Same Drug Testing Standards as Student Athletes

"[Student] athletes are being held to a higher standard than their teachers, principals and . . . School District Board of Trustees."

John L. Smith

John L. Smith is a columnist with the *Las Vegas Review-Journal*. In the viewpoint that follows, Smith contends that focusing drug detection and punishment programs exclusively on high school athletes is wrongheaded. Smith claims that athletes are unfairly singled out for testing when other students, who show more obvious symptoms of drug use, are not tested. In addition, Smith believes it is ridiculous to hold athletes to standards that are not imposed on faculty members. He believes it sends the wrong message to students; namely, that they are under suspicion simply for volunteering for sports.

AS YOU READ, CONSIDER THE FOLLOWING QUESTIONS:
1. Why does Smith think it is more appropriate to test police officers for drug use than to test student athletes?
2. According to the author, what kind of discipline process must Clark County firefighters undergo if they self-disclose a drug problem?
3. What does Smith think would be "refreshing" to implement regarding school drug testing?

Repeat after me, young people: Do as we say, not as we do.

That's the unspoken lesson being taught these days at Green Valley High School [in Clark County, Nevada], where Principal Jeff Horn has received high praise for implementing a random drug-testing program for his student-athletes. Horn's idea appears to be catching on with several other high schools now considering testing their student-athletes for drug use.

For a moment, forget whether such drug testing is effective. And never mind that the Clark County School District already offers an amazing variety of drug-prevention-related programs for students of all grades.

Look at it this way: Those athletes are being held to a higher standard than their teachers, principals and the Clark County School District Board of Trustees. And that sends a bell-ringing message.

Those student-athletes might not turn pro in their favorite sport. They might struggle with their math homework and have to cram to pass an American literature class. But thanks to this rule they'll always know the definition of hypocrisy.

Do as we say, not as we do.

Testing Civil Servants

Don't get me wrong. I'm not advocating increased drug testing, and I understand that teachers and administrators are protected by their contracts, but it does make sense for some occupations.

At Metro [Las Vegas police], officer Martin Wright tells me the department drug tests recruits and has random drug testing for officers. Tests also may be ordered based on a "reasonable suspicion of drug use or alcohol impairment," Wright says.

For cops, drug testing is smart. They carry guns, drive fast and have the power to arrest and take a life if necessary.

Clark County government employees in general aren't drug tested unless "there is reasonable cause that the employee is under the influence of a drug and/or alcohol," according to the current contract. Employees who carry commercial driver's licenses and operate large vehicles may be asked to take a drug test. A county employee involved in an accident while on duty also "may be required to undergo a drug and alcohol test" under certain conditions.

In case you're wondering, there's no drug testing for county commissioners or members of the City Council.

Clark County firefighters aren't allowed to use drugs, but they "shall not be subject to the disciplinary process" if they self-disclose their

Many people think college athletes are unfairly singled out for testing while other students who show more obvious symptoms of drug use are not tested.

"Are you willing to take a drug test and a vow of chastity while on school property?"

problem. In essence, the average firefighter works under a less aggressive drug policy than the one issued to a member of the Green Valley High football team.

Programs Are Already in Place

The School District has many needs, but it's not short of drug-abuse-prevention programs. Arlene Hummel heads the district's Safe and Drug Free Schools office, which coordinates programs throughout the system. She possesses the acronym-unraveling skills of a CIA code breaker.

Hummel brings in experts who educate students and teachers to the dangers of abusing drugs and alcohol. From DARE and Kids Are the Core, to the TARGET program and the upcoming SAVE substance abuse and anti-violence program, Hummel's office offers something for almost everyone.

"I think we're doing the best we can with the resources we have," Hummel says.

Although even sweeping anti-drug-abuse education programs don't ensure success, Metro narcotics Detective Brian Grammas and his partner Bruce Gentner teach the straight facts to hundreds of teachers and thousands of high school students each year.

"Hopefully, it gives them some knowledge," Grammas says, acknowledging the harsh realities.

Singling Out Athletes

A consistent set of rules would be refreshing, if you're into drug testing, doesn't it make more sense to randomly test those students who get poor grades and miss a lot of school?

Instead, the athletes, the students arguably the least likely to take drugs, are placed under suspicion.

Perhaps someone will argue the football team's backup punter has a more responsible duty than his English teacher. Maybe someone will contend the point guard for the girls' basketball team should be tested before the high school counselor in charge of assisting hundreds of students' lives. Superintendent Walt Rulffes wouldn't dream of trying.

"There is testing when an issue surfaces, and on occasion people are asked to test when there's some kind of evidence or allegation that there might be substance abuse present," Rulffes says.

But he readily acknowledges the irony of drug testing athletes in a system that doesn't test teachers or administrators.

Do as we say, not as we do.

> **EVALUATING THE AUTHOR'S ARGUMENTS:**
>
> In this viewpoint author John L. Smith poses the question of whether it makes more sense to perform drug tests on students who are often truant or are low achievers rather than on student athletes. Do you agree with Smith's suggestion? Why, or why not?

Facts About Athletes and Drug Use

Editor's note: These facts can be used in reports or papers to reinforce or add credibility when making important points or claims.

History

Associated Press (AP), *Sports Illustrated* (*SI*), and *USA Today* (*USAT*) provide the following important dates in the history of performance-enhancing drug use in sports:

- 1896: Welsh cyclist Arthur Linton dies during a race from Bordeaux to Paris. Though not listed as a cause of death, he supposedly was under the influence of the stimulant trimethyl. (*SI*)
- 1950s: After learning of the use of testosterone injections by the Russian weight-lifting team, US doctor John Ziegler devises the anabolic steroid methandrostenolone, which builds muscle without the dangerous side effects of pure testosterone. (*SI*)
- 1972: The International Olympic Committee (IOC) begins full-scale drug testing at the Olympics. (*USAT*)
- 1976: The IOC adds anabolic steroids to its list of banned substances. (*USAT*)
- 1985: Human growth hormone (HGH), a synthetic human growth hormone, is first produced. (*USAT*)
- 1988: Canadian sprinter Ben Johnson sets a world record and wins a gold medal in the 100-meter dash at the Seoul Olympics. He is quickly stripped of his medal after a urine test reveals the presence of an anabolic steroid in his body. (*SI*)
- 1999: The World Anti-Doping Agency (WADA), an independent drug testing organization, is formed through the IOC. (*SI*)
- 2003: Authorities investigate the Bay Area Laboratory Co-Operative (BALCO) and its founder, Victor Conte, as the maker and distributor of an undetectable steroid being used by several athletes. More than thirty athletes are ultimately subpoe-

naed to testify before a grand jury in San Francisco. Among those called to the stand are Olympic track-and-field champion Marion Jones and Major League Baseball (MLB) players Barry Bonds, Jason Giambi, and Gary Sheffield. (*SI*)

- 2004: A record twenty-four athletes are ousted for drug-related violations at the Athens Olympics. (*USAT*)
- 2005: Outfielder Jose Canseco publishes the tell-all book *Juiced: Wild Times, Rampant 'Roids, Smash Hits & How Baseball Got Big.* In it, he speaks of his own rampant steroid use and of alleged use by home run kings Mark McGwire and Sammy Sosa. (*SI*)
- 2006: After winning the Tour de France, US cyclist Floyd Landis tests positive for an illegal testosterone ratio. (*USAT*)
- 2007: *The Mitchell Report*, the findings of an independent investigation of steroid use in MLB, is released. The report names eighty-nine players who allegedly used steroids in their careers.
- 2008: Barry Bonds is charged with fifteen felony counts alleging he lied to a grand jury when he denied knowingly using performance-enhancing drugs and that he hampered the federal government's doping investigation. (*AP*)
- 2011: Barry Bonds is convicted of obstructing justice in the grand jury case.

Prevalence

WADA recorded eighty-eight rule violations among international athletic federations in 2010. The highest number of infractions (twenty-four) occurred in the federation for powerlifting.

In December 2010 MLB's Joint Drug Program reported that only 17 of 3,714 drug tests administered showed positive results that required discipline.

In September 2008 the *San Diego Union-Tribune* compiled its own version of the *Mitchell Report*, this time focusing on performance-enhancing drug use in American football. Starting in 1962, the paper linked 185 players to drug use, including four Hall of Famers.

According to the National Collegiate Athletic Association (NCAA), 68 out of 5,732 student athletes tested positive for banned substances in 2010.

In a January 2008 article in *Medicine & Science in Sports & Exercise*, Jay R. Hoffman, a professor at the College of New Jersey, reports that the use of anabolic steroids among eighth to twelfth graders ranges from 1.6 percent to 5.4 percent, a figure far lower than previous estimations.

The Centers for Disease Control and Prevention's 2009 Youth Risk Behavior Survey finds that 3.3 percent of ninth to twelfth graders admit to using steroids without prescription.

The National Institute on Drug Abuse states that steroids are often abused in one of three methods: cycling (using multiple doses of a steroid for a short period of time, stopping for a while, and then restarting the cycle); stacking (using more than one steroid at the same time); and pyramiding (slowly building up the dosage or number of steroids until a peak is reached, and then tapering off).

Effects

Steroids are typically taken orally or through injection. They are used to promote muscle growth and increase strength and endurance. According to the Partnership at Drugfree.org, steroids can also cause unwanted minor side effects such as acne, excess hair growth, and deepening of the voice. More serious side effects of steroid use include an increased risk of cancer, increased risk of heart and liver disease, jaundice, fluid retention, high blood pressure, changes in blood coagulation rates, increased risk of atherosclerosis (thickening and hardening of artery walls), and edema (swelling of the soft tissues of the extremities caused by fluid buildup).

HGH is injected into the body to promote muscle and bone growth and to regulate metabolism. According to the WebMD website, the side effects of HGH use may include nerve, muscle, or joint pain, edema, carpal tunnel syndrome, numbness and tingling of the skin, high cholesterol levels, increased risk of diabetes, and growth of cancerous tumors.

Erythropoietin (EPO) is injected into the body to promote healing and to increase the number of red blood cells (which can increase endurance). According to the Australian government's health website, unregulated EPO use can have dangerous side effects that include thickening of the blood, rapid increases in blood pressure, convulsions, influenza-like symptoms, bone aches and shivering following injection, skin reactions, allergy-like swelling at the site of injection, liver or pancreatic damage, and increased risk of developing liver or lymphatic cancers.

Responses

A March 2011 US Anti-Doping Agency poll revealed that 75 percent of about nine thousand people surveyed agreed that doping by athletes was a violation of ethics in sports.

A March 2009 ESPN/Seton Hall sports poll showed that more than 25 percent of the respondents believe that 50 percent of major leaguers, or more, are currently using HGH.

An April 2006 AP–AOL Sports poll reports that 53 percent of respondents believe MLB has fallen short on keeping the sport drug free.

A July 2008 *USA Today*/Gallup poll shows that when a track-and-field athlete sets a world record, more than one in three sports fans are suspicious that doping helped. The same poll found that more than one in five fans say they are suspicious of doping when a swimmer sets a world record.

A December 2007 Canadian Press Harris/Decima survey found that 17 percent of Canadians believe that many National Hockey League players use performance-enhancing drugs, while 36 percent say a fair number use them.

The NCAA requires at least one drug testing visit to every Division I and Division II school each year. In 2008–2009 the NCAA administered eleven thousand drug tests to student athletes.

Organizations to Contact

The editors have compiled the following list of organizations concerned with the issues debated in this book. The descriptions are derived from materials provided by the organizations. All have publications or information available for interested readers. The list was compiled on the date of publication of the present volume; the information provided here may change. Be aware that many organizations take several weeks or longer to respond to inquiries, so allow as much time as possible for the receipt of requested materials.

Anti-Doping Research, Inc. (ADR)
3873 Grand View Blvd., Los Angeles, CA 90066
(310) 482-6925
e-mail: info@antidopingresearch.org
website: www.antidopingresearch.org

ADR seeks to rid the sporting world of performance-enhancing drugs by conducting research to find new drugs, identify new ways old substances are being used to enhance performance, and develop new methods of detection. The ADR website provides extensive information about antidoping tactics with an antidoping timeline, educational videos, and access to a range of publications dealing with steroids and other topics.

Major League Baseball (MLB)
The Office of the Commissioner of Baseball, 245 Park Ave., 31st Fl., New York, NY 10167
(212) 931-7800 • fax: (212) 949-5654
website: www.mlb.com

The MLB is the official organization of the highest level of professional baseball in the United States and Canada. Under the direction of the commissioner, this entity works to ensure that everything from umpire crews to contracts and marketing is taken care of in order to execute the annual baseball season. As baseball has been one of the sports most publicly plagued with drug use by its players, the MLB website offers a special section titled "Drug Policy in Baseball," covering the ongoing prosecution of players for lying about their use of performance-enhancing drugs as well as current suspensions of players for drug use.

National Center for Drug Free Sport (Drug Free Sport)
2537 Madison Ave., Kansas City, MO 64108
(816) 474-8655 • fax: (816) 502-9287
e-mail: info@drugfreesport.com
website: www.drugfreesport.com

Drug Free Sport is a company dedicated to stopping the use of drugs by athletes through the development and implementation of reliable drug tests combined with educational programs on drug use in sports. The company provides an extensive database with information on dietary supplements and banned or prohibited drugs to member organizations. Additionally, the *Sports. Doping. Answers.* blog offers individuals current information about performance-enhancing drugs and supplements.

National Institutes of Health (NIH)
9000 Rockville Pike, Bethesda, MD 20892
(301) 496-4000
e-mail: nihinfo@od.nih.gov
website: www.nih.gov

As the research agency of the US Department of Health and Human Services, the NIH is responsible for conducting, funding, and disseminating the findings of medical research in all areas, including body systems, health and wellness, conditions and diseases, and procedures. Its research is also classified online by gender, age, and ethnicity/race. Within the NIH, the National Institute on Drug Abuse (NIDA) has focused its work on drug abuse and addiction, with extensive information on anabolic steroids. Publications on this topic include "NIDA Research Report: Anabolic Steroid Abuse" and "Steroid Abuse Is a High-Risk Route to the Finish Line." These and others can be accessed online.

The Partnership at Drugfree.org
352 Park Ave. South, 9th Fl., New York, NY 10010
(212) 922-1560 • fax: (212) 922-1570
e-mail: webmail@drugfree.org
website: www.drugfree.org

The Partnership at Drugfree.org is an organization seeking to help parents and families address their teen's drug use by educating them about the options available for treatment and intervention, connecting the families of teens addicted to drugs, and helping professionals in communities across the country to become more knowledgeable in their efforts to assist these individuals at the local level. While the partnership deals with all types of drugs, the site Play Healthy (www.playhealthy. drugfree.org) provides information and advice regarding the use of performance-enhancing drugs in sports. It contains videos, fact sheets, and an education presentation to inform visitors about the risks and pitfalls for athletes who use such drugs.

Play Clean Campaign

Butkus Foundation, c/o Ron Arp, 18920 NE 227th Ave., Brush Prairie, WA 98606
(360) 601-2991
website: www.iplayclean.org

The Play Clean Campaign was started by the Butkus Foundation (founded by National Football League Hall of Famer Dick Butkus, who wore number 51 for the Chicago Bears) to encourage student athletes to make the decision to pursue sports without the use of steroids or other performance-enhancing substances. The Play Clean website provides facts about steroids as well as a link to the *Fit Like 51* blog that offers current information on the regulation of supplements and tips for succeeding in sports without drugs.

Taylor Hooton Foundation (THF)

PO Box 2104, Frisco, TX 75034-9998
(972) 403-7300
website: www.taylorhooton.org

The THF was founded in 2004 following the death of seventeen-year-old Taylor Hooton, who committed suicide as a result of his anabolic steroid use. The foundation seeks to educate youth about the dangers of steroids in an effort to eventually eradicate steroid use entirely. On the THF website, visitors can browse steroid facts, find information about dietary supplements, and learn how to identify the signs of steroid abuse.

US Anti-Doping Agency (USADA)
5555 Tech Center Dr., Ste. 200, Colorado Springs, CO 80919-2372
(719) 785-2900 • fax: (719) 785-2001
e-mail: media@usada.org
website: www.usantidoping.org

USADA serves as the US Olympic movement's antidoping organization. In order to preserve the integrity of competition, the agency works to deter athletes from engaging in illicit substance use, to implement a sanctions program that punishes those athletes who seek to gain a competitive edge through the use of performance-enhancing substances, and to engage in cutting-edge research to ensure the application of the most comprehensive and up-to-date methods of doping control. Detailed information about banned and allowed substances can be found on the USADA website along with information about drug testing carried out by the agency. The biannual *Spirit of Sport* newsletter can be read online as well.

US Drug Enforcement Administration (DEA)
mailstop: AES, 8701 Morrissette Dr., Springfield, VA 22152
(202) 307-1000
website: www.justice.gov/dea

The DEA is the agency within the US Department of Justice charged with enforcing US drug laws and regulations and bringing those who disobey these laws to justice. In accordance with this mission, the DEA website provides information on all controlled substances in the United States. Testimony about steroids risks and their negative societal and personal impacts can be found online along with fact sheets, pictures of the drugs, and details about DEA operations targeting the illegal trade of these and other performance-enhancing drugs and supplements.

US Food and Drug Administration (FDA)
10903 New Hampshire Ave., Silver Spring, MD 20993-0002
(888) 463-6332
website: www.fda.gov

The FDA is the US government agency charged with overseeing and regulating the production, sale, and use of food and drug products in the United States. As such, the agency is in charge of everything from issuing recalls of products to providing congressional testimony, all in an effort to ensure the safety and health of American citizens. FDA information on performance-enhancing drugs includes the testimony "Bodybuilding Products and Hidden Steroids: Enforcement Barriers" and the consumer update "Warning on Body Building Products Marketed as Containing Steroids." These and many more can be read on the FDA website.

World Anti-Doping Agency (WADA)

Stock Exchange Tower, 800 Place Victoria, Ste. 1700,
Montreal, QC H4Z 1B7, Canada
(514) 904-9232 • fax: (514) 904-8650
e-mail: info@wada-ama.org • website: www.wada-ama.org

WADA has been working since its founding in 1999 to achieve an international doping-free sporting environment through a combination of scientific research, education campaigns, development of antidoping techniques, and observation of the World Anti-Doping Code. The WADA website offers detailed information about the World Anti-Doping Program, the antidoping community, and the organization's research. Details about the association's education and awareness programs directed at youth can be found online as well.

For Further Reading

Books

Assael, Shaun. *Steroid Nation: Juiced Home Run Totals, Anti-Aging Miracles, and a Hercules in Every High School; The Secret History of America's True Drug Addiction.* New York: ESPN, 2007. Tying sports to America's drive for success, journalist Assael reveals the country's addiction to steroids and the history of the drug in amateur and professional sports.

Beamish, Rob. *Steroids: A New Look at Performance-Enhancing Drugs.* Santa Barbara, CA: Praeger, 2011. After giving a thorough history of steroid use and drug scandals in sports, Beamish finds a ban on these drugs impractical. He advocates policies that seek to reduce the harms of steroid abuse while stopping short of outlawing use.

Carroll, Will, with William L. Carroll. *The Juice: The Real Story of Baseball's Drug Problems.* Chicago: Ivan R. Dee, 2005. Avoiding condemnation, Carroll uses interviews to provide a rationale for why baseball players seek advantages through performance-enhancing drugs. He weighs the benefits and dangers of drug use and discusses the impact of drugs on the game.

Fainaru-Wada, Mark, and Lance Williams. *Game of Shadows: Barry Bonds, BALCO, and the Steroids Scandal That Rocked Professional Sports.* New York: Gotham, 2006. *San Francisco Chronicle* reporters reveal the investigation of BALCO, the company accused of providing steroids to US athletes, and the numerous high-profile ballplayers linked to the scandal.

Hunt, Thomas M. *Drug Games: The International Olympic Committee and the Politics of Doping, 1960–2008.* Austin: University of Texas Press, 2011. An account of how antidoping policies were often ignored during the various Olympics that took place during the Cold War. Hunt shows how the desire to win prompted the United States and the Soviet Union to forgo creating any national drug policies for sport, leaving regulatory powers within the hands of specific sports authorities.

Mottram, David R., ed. *Drugs in Sport.* 5th ed. New York: Routledge, 2010. A traditional reference work that covers drug classifications, the history of doping, the antidoping movement, and the prevalence of drug use in sports.

Parisotto, Robin. *Blood Sports: The Inside Dope on Drugs in Sport.* Prahran, Victoria, Australia: Hardie Grant, 2006. The author traces the history of blood doping in sports and the lagging methods of detecting this form of performance enhancement. He also discusses the coming era of genetic doping, the heir to blood doping.

Pound, Richard W. *Inside Dope: How Drugs Are the Biggest Threat to Sports, Why You Should Care, and What Can Be Done About Them.* Mississauga, ON: John Wiley, 2006. Written by a former chairman of the World Anti-Doping Agency (WADA), this indictment of drug use in sports examines players' motives, the role of big business, and the encouragement of coaches to win at all costs. The book also emphasizes WADA's deterrence methods and the battle the organization fights to stay ahead of cheating.

Waddington, Ivan, and Andy Smith. *An Introduction to Drugs in Sport: Addicted to Winning?* New York: Routledge, 2009. The authors look into the reasons athletes are drawn to drugs and the role of doctors and trainers in encouraging or facilitating drug use. Waddington and Smith also analyze differing arguments on the appropriateness of drug bans based on the concept of violating the "spirit of sport."

Walsh, David. *From Lance to Landis: Inside the American Doping Controversy at the Tour de France.* New York: Ballantine, 2007. Walsh examines the role of drug use in the Tour de France cycling race as well as the allegations that eventually brought down 2006 winner Floyd Landis and continue to swirl around the career of seven-time champion Lance Armstrong.

Periodicals

Aldhouse, Peter. "Olympic Cheats: Creating a Culture That Rejects Doping," *New Scientist,* August 2, 2008.

Battista, Judy. "N.F.L. Said to Be Closer to Testing for H.G.H.," *New York Times,* August 3, 2011.

Brown, W. Miller. "The Case for Perfection," *Journal of the Philosophy of Sport,* Fall 2009.

Burch, Druin. "Blood Sports," *Natural History,* June 2011.

Callaway, Ewen. "Sports Doping: Racing Just to Keep Up," *Nature,* July 21, 2011.

Dowbiggin, Bruce. "Playing Fair," *Beaver: Exploring Canada's History,* December 2009/January 2010.

Dunn, Matthew, et al. "Drug Testing in Sport: The Attitudes and Experiences of Elite Athletes," *International Journal of Drug Policy,* July 2010.

Economist. "For the Joy of It," August 2, 2008.

Epstein, David, and George Dohrmann. "What You Don't Know Might Kill You," *Sports Illustrated,* May 18, 2009.

Friedmann, Theodore, Olivier Rabin, and Mark S. Frankel. "Gene Doping and Sport," *Science,* February 5, 2010.

Gillis, Charlie. "Cheaters Will Always Be with Us," *Maclean's,* August 13, 2007.

Henry, Marcus. "Why Is Congress Picking on Baseball?," *New York Amsterdam News,* February 12, 2009.

Kingsbury, Alex. "A Gamble on Substance," *U.S. News & World Report,* August 6, 2007.

Kotler, Steven. "Juicing 3.0," *Popular Science,* August 2008.

Miah, Andy. "Rethinking Enhancement in Sport," *Annals of the New York Academy of Sciences,* 2006.

Murray, T.H. "Doping in Sport: Challenges for Medicine, Science and Ethics," *Journal of Internal Medicine,* August 2008.

Pitock, Todd. "Pumping Irons," *Forbes,* December 10, 2007.

Roberts, Selena, and David Epstein. "The Case Against Lance Armstrong," *Sports Illustrated,* January 24, 2011.

Shermer, Michael. "The Doping Dilemma," *Scientific American,* April 2008.

Socher, Abraham. "No Game for Old Men," *Commentary,* March 2008.

Verducci, Tom. "The Short Goodbye," *Sports Illustrated,* April 18, 2011.

Von Drehle, David. "The Moment," *Time,* February 23, 2009.

Walsh, Mark. "Random Drug Testing Found Unconstitutional in Washington State," *Education Week,* March 19, 2008.

Websites

Association Against Steroid Abuse (www.steroidabuse.com). This website is dedicated to warning against the dangers of steroid abuse. It has several sections detailing the effects of steroids, legal aspects of steroid use, and steroid use in sports, among others.

Baseball's Steroid Era (www.baseballssteroidera.com). This archive of documents, timelines, lists, and other articles related to steroid use in Major League Baseball was compiled by George Godfrey. The purpose of the site is to bring together various media resources that cover this significant aspect of baseball history.

ESPN Drugs and Sports Special (http://espn.go.eom/special/s /drugsandsports). A special eight-week analysis of the influence and impact of drugs on sports, ESPN's website examines the prevalence and use of steroids, amphetamines, alcohol, and other drugs.

Mayo Clinic (www.mayoclinic.com). The Mayo Clinic website provides an overview of the risks of performance-enhancing drugs as well as the impact of these drugs on teenagers. The staff notes the side effects of steroids, human growth hormone, and erythropoietin and discusses these drugs' attractions and risks to athletes.

National Collegiate Athletic Association Drug Testing Program (www.steroidabuse.com). The NCAA compiles a useful list of banned substances, drug testing policies, and statistical results of annual testing. The website also offers an educational video on drug abuse and drug testing in college sports.

Steroid Law (www.steroidlaw.com). Managed by attorney Rick Collins, this site offers legal advice as well as information on steroid use and abuse. Collins argues that both the harmful and positive effects of steroids are commonly exaggerated in the media; his mission is to compile various articles and arguments that illustrate how complex the issue of steroid use is and how laws might be reformed to address that complexity.

Index

poses health threat to athletes, 51–55
side effects of, *54*
Hummel, Arlene, 114, 115
Hurd, Zack, 95
Hyperplasia, 47

I
Illston, Susan, 69
Insulin-like growth factor, 25–26
International Cycling Union, 27
International Olympic Committee (IOC), 7, 64–65
ban on human growth hormone by, 55

J
Johnson, Ben, 20, 28, 77
Jones, Marion, 96, *98*

L
Lanier, Randy, 71

M
Major League Baseball (MLB), 58, 109
initiates penalties for steroid-using players, 71
Maradona, Diego, 82
Marijuana, 86, 88, 107, 110
support for legalization of, *89*
Marinello, Sal V., 46
Medscape (website), 33
Millar, Anthony P., 8, 60
Mitten, Matthew J., 8

MLB. *See* Major League Baseball
Moses, Ed, 75
Murray, T.H., 38
Muscle, human growth hormone and, 47–48
Mutu, Adrian, 82

N
National Center for Drug-Free Sport, 106
National Collegiate Athletic Association (NCAA), 96
drug testing by, 106
drug testing policy of, *108*
drug use in, by division, *102*
substances banned by, *97*
variation in drug testing policies among schools in, 105
weaknesses in drug testing programs of, 106, 109
National Football League (NFL), 7–8, 109
National Institute on Drug Abuse (NIDA), 58
NCAA. *See* National Collegiate Athletic Association
New York Times (newspaper), 8
NFL (National Football League), 7–8, 109
NIDA (National Institute on Drug Abuse), 58
Nielsen, Mark, 92

O
O'Connor, Johnny, 11

Picture Credits

© AP Images/Tony Avelar, 70

© AP Images/Damian Dovarganes, 56, 107

© AP Images/Keystone, Walter Bieri, 90

© AP Images/Lefteris Pitarakis, 63

© AP Images/Sang Tan, 83

© AP Images/Andy Wong, 32

© Denis Balibouse/Reuters/Landov, 26

© Biophoto Associates/Photo Researchers, Inc., 53

© Russell Boyce/Reuters/Landov, 78

Gale/Cengage Learing, 14, 28, 49, 54, 65, 69, 84, 89, 97, 102, 108

© John Giles/PA Photos/Landov, 101

© PCN Photography/Alamy, 13

© RIA Novosti/Photo Researchers, Inc., 94

© Doug Steley/Alamy, 43

© Victor Habbick Visions/Photo Researchers, Inc., 10

© Craig Warga/NY Daily News Archive via Getty Images, 98

© Jared Wickerham/Getty Images, 113